Off to College
in a Cattle Truck
Stories I've heard while traveling
with Joe and others

By the Possum Trot Storyteller

Ray Lipps

Ray Lipps

ISBN:10:1500541087
ISBN-13:978-1500541088

DEDICATION

This book is dedicated to all the characters
I have known and to Jim and Dinah Taylor, without
whose leadership the future of the University of the
Cumberlands would be uncertain.

CONTENTS

ACKNOWLEDGMENTS

Without the assistance of Susan Alexander, there would be no book from me. Thank you, Susan, for helping me realize a dream. Pat and I want to thank Dr. Monroe Trout for doing the wonderful painting that was used for the book cover. It has been our privilege to be friends with Monroe and Sandy, whom we met because of our mutual interest in the University of the Cumberlands and the arts. Thanks to my wife, Pat, who read the manuscript many times in an effort to correct any grammatical mistakes. Thanks to my twin brother's good friend, Dr. Roland Mullins, who about two years ago suggested I write a book about my family. While I did not do the kind of book that he was suggesting to me, it was the first time I had thought about writing. Thanks to my first cousin, John (Jay) Lipps, the unofficial historian of Possum Trot. Thanks to Dave Bergman for his encouragement and his loyalty to me personally. I would be remiss if I did not thank my brother, Ab (a true character) for providing all the stories about him that I've used in this book. In many ways, he is the most successful of the three of us. And thanks to all the characters it has been my privilege to know.

Dr. Ray Lipps
Possum Trot Storyteller

The House by the Side of the Road

There are hermit souls that live withdrawn
In the place of their self-content;
There are souls like stars, that dwell apart,
In a fellowless firmament;
There are pioneer souls that blaze the paths
Where highways never ran –
But let me live by the side of the road
And be a friend to man.
Let me live in a house by the side of the road
Where the race of men go by –
The men who are good and the men who are bad,
As good and as bad as I.
I would not sit in the scorner's seat
Nor hurl the cynic's ban –
Let me live in a house by the side of the road
And be a friend to man.

Sam Walter Foss

INTRODUCTION

At the end of World War II, my father, Joe Lipps, met my mother at Staten Island General Hospital. He was a military policeman with the U.S. Army who had the job of taking soldiers home who were unable to travel alone. My mother, Susan Mahler, was the person who checked these men out of the hospital. They were married in 1945 and moved back to Joe's father's home in eastern Kentucky. Susan, who grew up in New York City and was well educated, prepared herself for the move by reading two books by Jesse Stuart: "Taps for Private Tussie" and "The Thread That Ran So True." After Joe was unable to find work, he packed up his new wife and moved to Cincinnati and found work as a carpenter.

On June 19, 1947, twins – Ralph and Ray – were born to the couple. After this they moved to Possum Trot, Kentucky, where a year and a day later a third son, Abner, was born.

Susie was a writer for the local newspaper, the Sentinel Echo, so writing seemed inevitable for someone who had a mother who wrote and who grew up in a place named Possum Trot. The problem was I wasn't a writer. Instead, I told stories, so I became the 'Possum Trot Storyteller.' In the following pages I've told eighty or so stories that I found interesting. I doubt that I will come this way again, so enjoy.

MULE STORY NUMBER ONE

Our family doctor's name is Robert Alan Rice. On a recent visit to his office, my wife asked him if anyone ever called him by his first name, Robert, since we have always referred to him as Dr. Alan Rice. His response was adamant: "Absolutely no way, as it was a bone of contention between my parents from the beginning. My mother wanted to name me Mark Anthony, and my father wouldn't agree to such a name. After I was born, I had to be named before they could take me out of the hospital, so finally they agreed on Robert Alan. But my father realized all the mules in the county were called 'Bob' or 'Jim,' and that my Robert would be shortened to Bob. So whenever they hollered at the mule – get up, Bob, or whatever the command — I would think they were calling me. Therefore, I had to be called 'Alan.'"

POSSUM TROT

Let me tell you three things that affected me and my brothers' early life. I've told this story many times, but I want to get it right *every time.*

My mother came from New York City. She was born Jewish. She never practiced; she became a Baptist, she married my father and they moved to Laurel County. Now my mother was the most intelligent person anybody ever met or anybody ever knew of. She wrote for the local newspaper for 30 years. And her goal in life was to get on one of those "Truth or Consequences" talk shows where they ask you questions. She would never have missed a question. She knew 'em all, and there's some question whether she helped my younger brother write some term papers when we were in college.

But she was loved by everybody far and near, and the day she died, there was an article by her in the paper that day, and then there were two other articles written by as graceful writers as she was about her, and they said she was probably the most famous person who ever lived in our

3

county. We got letters from all over the world when she died. I judge everything and everybody by her.

My parents altered our lives by three different circumstances. The first one is they never required we call them anything but by first name. So when we started elementary school, we got harassed because we called them Joe and Susie, you know. People thought we didn't respect 'em; teachers asked us to change over. That was the first big mistake that everybody thought we made.

The second was we had no middle names. Ralph and I were twins, so they got our social security messed up. Our last numbers are just one digit apart, so what happened is some years he got my income and other years I got his income. The reason they have those guards settin' in the social security office is for deals like this. For 40 years we tried to get this straightened out, and we never got it straightened out. So you got two pretty bad things startin' out, but let me tell you the worst one.

When Ralph and I were six years old, Ab was five years old. It was two miles to walk to where we went to school, and my twin and I started out up the road to go to school that first day, and Ab started cryin', and Joe said, "C'mon back, boys, you can all go next year."

So there we was twiddlin' our thumbs waitin' for us to be genius auctioneers and chemists and CEOs of mental health centers and stuff like that; we twiddled our thumbs while my brother got to be six years old. Of course, when we finally got there, we had all three of us sitting in the same seat and taking the same classes all the way up through college and grad school, and all of the hassles that go with that. Plus, there's some good things; when we were in grade school nobody picked on us, you know, 'cuz there was three of us in the same grade. There was gonna be an ass kickin' if you messed with the Lipps boys.

So recently I told my brother Ralph that it occurred to me that Ab has cost me and him at least a hundred thousand dollars apiece by not startin' school on time, and I think we probably oughta sue him. And about half an hour later my younger brother called me, and he said, "What the hell's goin' on down there with you guys?" I said, "I don't know what you're talkin' about, Ab." And he said, "Well, Ralph just called me and said, 'You little wimp, your cryin' up there cost Ray and me a hundred thousand dollars apiece, and we're gonna sue your ass.' What's that about?"

~ ~ ~

Every elementary school in America probably has a gang. Ours at Campground School, where the three of us went to school, had a gang, and that gang was called the Zero Holler Gang. Now the way we got our name, our leader was Orville Hammock. He started the Zero Holler Gang, and the reason it was called Zero Holler is when we came back to school in the fall, there would be these ragweeds down along the edge of the school property and these ragweeds would be seven or eight feet tall and about a half inch through at the bottom of 'em, and we took our pocketknives and we would make a path down through to the center of 'em. Then we'd cut this big ol' circle out, thus the Zero Holler Gang. And we'd go down there at break; this was somewhere in the vicinity where you could see the girls' toilet, and that was a big thing in those days, just to be able to see the women's bathroom, you know. But anyway, that's another story.

The Zero Holler Gang was made up of Abner Lipps, Ralph Lipps, Ray Lipps, Orville Hammock, James Overbay, Willis Jackson, Paul Williams and Maynard Snyder. Maynard was the toughest person we knew. He could hold a firecracker in his fingers and let it go off in his hand. Now he did this on purpose; you didn't mess with Maynard Snyder.

The Zero Holler Gang had no agenda. We'd sometimes go down there and eat our lunches and if we had an infraction with somebody, you'd go down there to, you know, home base, and your friends would help guard you so somebody didn't beat you up or something like that. Se we were truly a gang, and to my knowledge there was never an opposing gang, and we never had any gang wars, but we were truly a gang. The Zero Holler Gang.

CAMP GROUND SCHOOL

GRADES 3-4

1957 - 1958

I am the best looking boy in the class; second row, second from the left.

~~~

In my early life, I remember a round TV with a crack down the center of it and some chips around that crack that kinda changed the look of everything that came on the screen. We watched the TV for the news; we went to bed around 7:30 or 8 o'clock in the evening and got up at 6 o'clock in the morning. It was the last thing we saw goin' to bed and the first thing in the mornin' when we got up.

We watched Cas Walker, which came in from Knoxville. If you had a tall antenna in Possum Trot up on top of a hill, you could get Channel 10 and Channel 6 from Knoxville, and Dolly Parton would be singin' on the Cas Walker Show. Cas Walker was a grocer in Knoxville who was very political, and he had some exotic ideas about how the government ought to be run, and he spewed them on the airwaves every morning of the week, and Dolly Parton came in and sang in between his political rants.

We watched Roy Rogers and Gene Autry, and we churned butter while we watched them. My little brother Abner spent an inordinate amount of his time watching Roy Rogers and Gene Autry, which he now denies, and there's not many witnesses left alive, but my twin brother Ralph and I agree he spent more time watchin' TV than he did workin', while we worked more than we watched TV, we thought. I think my brother still has the round TV along with every nickel and dollar he's ever made

So for you folks who now have these big, exotic pieces of equipment, it's fascinating to go back and look at the archaic pieces of equipment we were able to get voices over the air with.

~~~

When I was a young kid, one of the greatest occasions was at Christmastime when my uncle and my aunt sent a great, huge box and we had to take the wagon over to the post office to pick it up. It was a box like 4 by 4 by 4, filled with things for Christmas for the country boys. The city folks sent us gifts each year in my memory until we were probably out of high school.

One of the things they sent us were these really fancy cap pistols. There was a double holster for the guns, one on each hip, and they were the rage of Campground School, where we went to elementary school. We wore 'em to school every day, as did most other boys with their own cap pistols, you know, and, lo and behold, I got home one day and one of my pistols was missing out of its holster. Somehow during the day I had lost it.

I had no idea where it was; I spent the next few days lookin' for it, worrying my parents would find out I'd lost it. I went back and retraced all the places I'd been, and I looked and I spent a couple of sleepless nights worrying about it. I mean this was big time serious stuff; I had lost one of those precious pistols that my uncle had sent especially to me. I just couldn't believe I'd lost it, and I couldn't believe I couldn't find it anywhere. I wanted to tell my parents about it but I kept puttin' it off thinkin' I'd find it any day now.

Well, a week went by and I did not find it, and it was about two o'clock in the morning and I was layin' awake thinkin' about it, and I just couldn't take it any longer. I had to tell my father that I lost that pistol and take whatever was comin', which I was pretty sure wasn't gonna be good. So I went in their bedroom, and I put my hand on his shoulder and shook it and woke him up, and I said, "Joe, I lost one of my pistols," and he said, "That's OK, son, go back to sleep." And that, I don't care who you are, is how you spell relief.

~ ~ ~

Every once in a while at night when I'm half asleep, my mind wanders over some of the dangerous things I've done in my life. And one of the most dangerous things that we ever did growin' up was we played this game called Annie Over. That's where you have a ball and you throw it over the building, and the people on the other side, if they catch it, may take that ball and run it around the other side and tag people with it until everybody gets tagged out. And whoever had people standing at the end won the contest.

Now it was a well-known fact that some of us cheated, that whether we caught the ball or not, we grabbed it and ran around the building and tagged people. And we may have threatened people who did not join us in that endeavor with harm if they told anybody or didn't come along with us.

Now the thing that is scarin' me sometimes is every now and then one of us would pick up a brick and throw it over the building. Can you imagine standin' there waitin' for a ball to come over the buildin' and here comes a brick. It took total concentration to keep from being killed on the playground. Lo these many years later, I still worry what would've happened if that brick had hit somebody.

~~~

Whenever it stormed — lightnin', thunder — a couple of our neighbors would come down to our house, and they'd sit on the front porch and look worried. And when the storm was over and they left, I asked Joe, "Why do they come down to our house; why do they do that?" And Joe told me, "They're afraid of lightnin'; they're afraid lightnin' will strike their house and it will kill 'em and burn their house down."

And I said, "Why do they come down here?" And he said, "I just told you; they're frightened. They think that lightnin' might strike their house, and they come down here." And I said, "Let me think about this, Joe." Now I was about 7 or 8 years old, you know. "If lightnin' was gonna strike their house and they came down to our house, it seems to me that would entice lightnin' to strike OUR house just to get them. Let's run 'em off."

He would say, "No, no, you're wrong, son." He said, "Lightnin's not gonna strike their house OR our house. It MAY strike our house, but we don't know; nobody can know where lightnin's gonna strike but God." So every time the storm would come up, these folks would come to the house, and every time they come to our house we would have this discussion. And we'd have it to the point he'd eventually tell me he didn't want to discuss it anymore.

But as a result of setting out on the front porch when it was lightnin' and thunderin' and all, I don't think any of the three brothers are too worried about lightnin'. In fact, there's a beauty about it, and we did sit out on the front porch and watch it, which probably was not prudent. Anyway we never solved the problem of convincing these people that lightnin' could strike 'em as well at our house as it could at their house.

~ ~ ~

Saturday night rasslin' was a big, big deal in Possum Trot. There were only a few TVs in Possum Trot in my first memories, and our next-door neighbor had a TV, and every Saturday night we went up to their house early in the evening, and we would watch rasslin'. Everybody seemed to be animated during these wrestling matches. Some of us kids, we were up practicing our rasslin' moves like the guys on TV. There would be Gorgeous George, which would be suspect today, but Gorgeous George was a gorgeous guy who was a rassler, and the whole community enjoyed rasslin'. At this point in our lives and careers, it's difficult to admit that we were actually participants in watching rassling; we would deny it now that we did that.

Possum Trot was a place where many people thought rasslin' was real and the moon landing was fake. They did not believe that anybody had walked on the moon, but rasslin' was real. And rasslin' was an integral part of our early lives. It took us a quarter of a century to figure out that rasslin' was not real. That was a big, big disappointment to many people in Possum Trot.

~~~

Out on the farm we were probably the first people in Possom Trot to have electric fences. And as time went on these fences became very sophisticated. They had a weed burner, you know; when a weed grew up and got into the wire, you would think that would ground it, but it would just burn it off; that's how sophisticated these electric fences was. So at one point it wadn't workin' on some portion on our farm a long ways from the batteries that made it hot; it went half a mile around our farm, you know, the wire did; and my brother Ab was over a long way from the barn over on the hill, and Joe would tell him to touch the wire — we have a very sophisticated way of telling if the wire was hot; it was called 'touch it' — and if it knocked your damn arm out of place, it was on.

So anyway, we were in that testing mode, and Ab was saying the electric was not getting over to where he was. So I was about 100 yards up the fence and so he would tell me to touch it, so I had on these big ol' rubber boots. My theory was the electric would not go through them, you know. And so, I was correct. He would tell me to touch it, and I would lean over and grab that wire with my fist, and he could see me, you know, and he would think, well, it must be off here. So he'd reach out and touch it where it came out of the box, and it would just flatten him. I got him to touch that wire about four or five times, and he finally got wise. He said, "Put your hand on the ground, and touch that wire." And I said, "Nah, we don't have to do that, do we?" And he said, "Yep, put your hand on the ground. I wanna see that hand on the ground." So I put my hand on the ground and touched it, and it turned me a somersault, you know. That's how we tested whether the electric was on on the fence.

~~~

Our next door neighbor in Possum Trot was a preacher named Richmond Hammock. Richmond had this habit of going every Saturday night over to Keavy, Kentucky, to a small auction they had over there. They were some of the first auctions I ever went to, and it started me on a lifelong pursuit of working in auctions, buying and selling; my whole career has been in selling art at auctions, with very few interruptions.

Richmond loved to go to these auctions. There were two auctions, really; one on a weeknight in London and the one in Keavy on Saturday night, and we'd go to both of those. He'd invite me to ride with him over to auctions. So, they would sell these box lots, and I would buy a box lot from each of those auctions. So twice a week I would get a box of stuff for a dollar or fifty cents, something like that, and I would take it home.

I was a budding builder in those days, I was my own construction boss, so I went down to one of the barns, and I went in the corner and I built me a floor and put some walls on it, and put some slabs and wood on it, wherever I could find me some wood, and I built me this little room which was about six-by-six, and I put me a big old padlock in it, you know, and all my treasures that I'd buy at auction I'd put in that room and store 'em and keep 'em as an investment in the future. There was a day that I realized it might not be an investment in the future; it might more likely be a pile of junk. And Joe helped me come to that conclusion along the way.

I don't know if that little building is still out there at the farm; I haven't been out there to look in the last few years, but it may still be there. In fact, if it is still there, there may be some very valuable antiques in it that I got out of those box lots. That's the way people who go to auctions think, just like I'm telling you. We never give up the idea that someday we're going to find something in one of those box lots that's going to bring wealth to the whole family.

But I'm forever indebted to Preacher Richmond Hammock for introducing me to going to auctions, and for many years I joined him on Saturday night to go to an auction event.

He enjoyed them as much as I did, and he didn't buy much more than I did. But we really had a good time.

~ ~ ~

On Saturday night my parents and my two brothers and I would go up to the next-door neighbor's house where we would watch rasslin' on in the early afternoon, and then we had this tremendously aggressive, competitive rook game. People got mad at each other, people hollered and screamed, people won and people lost, and there were chickens wanderin' through the house, and sometimes they would feed 'em part of a beer and there would be drunk chicken wanderin' through the house.

My brothers and I were not allowed to play, but we could hang around and watch the game, and later on we would watch "Bonanza" or "Rawhide" or "The Virginian"; all these were shows that were on on Saturday night prime time. So as kids we got to watch the rook games, and then we would go and watch these shows while they played a little bit longer, and it was a Saturday night well spent when we weren't hunting or going to antiques auctions or things like that.

Some of the most wonderful memories we have are of the Saturday night rook games. We played to 500, we all cheated. Everybody that played rook in our community was an expert at the game of rook, which basically made it a mechanical game – whoever got the best cards won; nobody made any mistakes in how you played the game.

Now if you threw cheating in the picture, then that changed the whole evening because that meant anybody could win. No matter what you got in your cards, if you cheated you could probably win. So cheating was a big deal; we all did it from time to time in rook, and it prepared us for those long rook games in college when we were snowed in and played to 10,000.

Now getting caught cheating meant a sentence almost like death; if you got caught cheating at rook, man, you would do anything; you were just the lowest kind of citizen. And most of the citizens of Possum Trot thought we were on a higher route than that, but Saturday night rook and cheating was important, and not getting caught was paramount to a good evening.

~~~

As you know by now, we grew up on a farm. We raised cattle. We had a bull, and we had a neighbor who had a cow. And this was absolutely the smartest cow that any of us ever knew about. Because our neighbor did not have a bull, and the cost of getting the cow pregnant was five bucks. And every year that cow managed to get over in our field about the time that she was lookin' for some love, and we had a bull that was known to provide the kind of love that she needed, and this happened maybe eight or ten times, you know. So there were some smart cattle in our part of the country.

~~~

Our neighbor the Rev. Richmond Hammock did not have a gun, and he had this skunk in his barn, eating all the eggs and killing chickens. So he came up and asked Joe if he'd come down and shoot the skunk. So I begged Joe to let me do it; I was about 10 or 12 years old, and I went with him down to Richmond's house, and he told us the skunk was in the barn at the time, and I was relentless asking if I could do it or not, so he finally agreed.

So he placed me about 100 feet from the barn, and he said, "Now don't shoot the skunk till he gets a little distance from the barn because it'll make it stink around there for a long time." He said, "Do you understand what I'm sayin'?" I said, "Yes, I understand."

So he went in the barn to kinda shake the skunk up and get him movin' toward this hole he came in and out of. So I was standin' there waitin' on him, you know, very intently, and givin' it all my attention. So anyway, the skunk stuck his head out of the hole where he came in and out, and I shot him right there in that hole. And, boy, did it stink. And Joe looked at me and said, "That's not what I asked you to do. I believe you didn't hear me."

~ ~ ~

When I was growing up in Possum Trot, there were some routines we got into as citizens of Possum Trot. To my knowledge there were 22 families that lived there. And one of those families was made up of distant cousins that lived next door to us. One of our distant relatives had married a man named Willie Langdon.

Willie Langdon and I became fast friends. He was much older than I was. I was just a young kid, and he was a carpenter. Willie Langdon was one of those folks who has lived a very good life. He was a carpenter, he was talented and intelligent. And he and I spent a lot of time together. We worked together, and on Friday nights we went coon hunting. Some people thought we went fox hunting since the dogs ran foxes most of the evening.

We would leave in the early evening; it was always hot, and we would leave before it cooled down. It would be hot, and therefore we did not anticipate it being any other way. So we would not wear enough clothes. We would not have a coat, and we would walk and walk and walk and walk and then we'd pass by somebody with an apple tree and so we got us an apple, and maybe we took a candy bar, and we would listen to these dogs; we would sit up against a tree and listen to these hounds.

And it was like listening to a really good quartet. We had four or five dogs; we had dogs with big ol' heavy, deep voices and dogs with really high voices. It was a wonderful experience. We assumed that they were running coons and not running possums or foxes. But many times we would go to the tree where the dogs had treed something, and what we treed was a possum or something like that. Our dogs were good dogs and they did the best they could, but from time to time they had to have retraining sessions.

It was on these nights that Willie and I solved some of the world's problems. He thought that I was pretty intelligent, and I knew that he was intelligent, and we knew that our conversation was important to mankind in general. I'm telling you this story so you will understand how wonderful it is, on a night like that night, after you've sat there and regretted not having a coat and covered yourself up with leaves, and by the time you got home you would ask yourself why am I doing this? Why I am going coon hunting and freezing to death when all I had to do was just bring a jacket and be very comfortable. And I vowed the next Friday night I would do just that, I would bring a jacket. But most of the time it never did happen; I continued to practice the same mistake over and over and over again.

But it did allow me one of the great sensations of my life. When I would get home and go to my bed and get under a pile of covers it was always the most wonderful sensation in the world, to come home to my house and get warm again. And in the morning I would contemplate never doing it again, and then next Friday night there I was again, doing the same thing. That was life in Possum Trot.

~ ~ ~

This is the famous goat story, and it involves Richmond Hammock, who lived next door to us. Ralph and Ab and I, when we'd go to these auction sales, from time to time Joe would let us buy something, a pony or something along those lines, and one time we were at an auction, and they had this big ol' huge goat.

So we asked Joe could we pool our money; I think it was three dollars, a dollar apiece we got together, and we bought this goat. And we took it out to our farm and turned it loose. There was no keeping it fenced in; it went anywhere it wanted to, and there was no way to control its behavior, and so one afternoon Richmond came up to have a conference with Joe, and he said, "I hate to do this; I know those boys love that goat and everything, but this goat is runnin' across my porch at two and three o'clock in the morning, and it's wakin' us up, and we can't get any rest."

And of course Joe had an immediate family meeting, and he said, "You know, one of my goals in life is to always get along with my neighbors; that's something I've tried to teach you boys, and this goat has to go, or you have to come up with some plan to keep it from runnin' across Richmond's porch. I'm just not gonna tolerate that any longer. It has to be solved today!"

So the way we solved that as boys, you know, this is what we came up with: We went out and cut this tree down that was about three inches across at the bottom of it and we took a piece of rope and tied it to the goat and then tied it to the tree. So the goat could pull that tree very slowly across the field, so he could get a new spot to graze but he couldn't pull it very fast and he couldn't go very far with it.

About two weeks later Richmond made another trek up to our house, and he told Joe, he said, "Joe, we gotta do something about this goat." And Joe said, "I thought we did do something about it; we tied it to that tree." And he said, "That's what I'm talking about. That goat is draggin' that tree back across my porch now." So the goat had to go. That's the famous goat story.

~~~

This story is about Orville Hammock. Orville Hammock was an interestin' fella; he was the founder of the Zero Holler Gang. He kept it alive all these years, he talks about it at every reunion; as far as I know his claim to fame was he was the organizer of the Zero Holler Gang.

Orville was probably the only person from Laurel County who ever rode a bicycle to the Cincinnati area, and he did it on a regular basis. He was also the chief Grits salesman in our county; he sold more Grits than anybody else. Grit was a magazine; you got paid a nickel or something to sell 'em.

When we graduated from high school he had a car, I believe it was a '49 Ford, and he made it look like a Dominicker chicken; he went all over it and put these black and white spots all over it; it was kind of gray; and it looked like a chicken.

For 25 years or so the Class of '66 got together on an often basis; many times we had gatherings of the survivors of the

Class of '66, and Orville could be counted on to provide entertainment because he and his girlfriend or wife, whichever it was, were usually in high spirits, and they usually ended up mad at each other, and that was entertainment. Lo and behold, the last time we had a reunion Orville and his wife were stone-cold sober, and I'll tell you this, it is one man's opinion, but I believe the reunions we have in the future will not be the same without everyone being a little bit tipsy.

~~~

I remember the day that my parents got a chain letter. It was a rather threatening chain letter. They had never heard of anything like this before that time.

The letter said that if you do not pass this along to ten other people, something terrible will happen to you and your family. They didn't quite believe it, but it worried them for three or four weeks, about if they didn't eventually mail it out, what would happen to them. It had a couple of religious quotes in it, which was even more bothersome – that somebody would put something religious in a letter like that, so it was the talk of our home for maybe three weeks.

When I compare that experience to today, you would probably get a letter like that now on the computer, and you could look it up and maybe understand it better. But in those days, we didn't have a computer or anybody to help us with it, and nobody had ever gotten a chain letter before in Possum Trot.

Three or four families in Possum Trot got this chain letter, so we figured it must be somebody who knows some of us, and then there came the really important question: If we were going to adhere to the letter's request and save ourselves from all the wrath which would come down on us, then we had to pick ten other poor souls out there to send this letter to. And that would have been tragic, for my family to pick out ten other people who'd begin to worry. It appeared that eventually everybody in Possum Trot would get one of these letters and we'd all be worryin' together, and maybe we could call a town – not a town, we were never a town – a community meeting to discuss what we could do about this and try to figure out exactly who put out the letter. As I remember no other letter got such an important position in our lives for three weeks or so.

~ ~ ~

When I was growing up in the latter part of high school, we started using electric fences. Animals could not see this fence, but they knew where it was at, and they avoided that area almost to the point of death. Whenever we had the cattle in that electric fence, we'd take the fence down and it was kinda hilarious to watch us get the cattle to cross where that line used to be. They could not see if it was there or not, so they would not cross, and you had to get 'em down and drag' 'em across it.

We had a dog named Bowser. We named that dog after a family named Bowser who lived just outside the area known as Possum Trot. They lived in Campground, which was the next community over, but we named our dog after that family , and I guess we were in college before somebody alerted us that Bowser was actually a dog's name.

Bowser was a little black dog, and he was always happy, and he was inside this fence on the day we were takin' the fence down and – this is a cruel story, I've lived all these years without telling this story, but it's a pretty good story — and without thinking, I said, "Come 'ere, Bowser," and Bowser went runnin' under that wire, and his tail was stickin' up, and it bobbed the wire, and I didn't actually intend for him to get shocked like that, but his tail was stickin' up and he got shocked, and for the rest of his life whenever you said "Come 'ere, Bowser," he turned around and headed the other way. It was almost like we trained him.

SUSIE

Once the decision was made by my father and mother to get married, my mother knew that she would be moving from Staten Island, New York, to Doublecreek, Clay County, Manchester, Kentucky. The middle of the mountains, the heart of Appalachia.

She was a lifelong reader, so she began to read up on what life was like in Doublecreek, Kentucky. There was a young author who lived in Greenup County, Kentucky, whose name was Jesse Stuart, and Jesse Stuart had had a very successful book. He had written a book called "The Thread That Runs So True." It was about teaching when the students were older than he, and he was a great author.

So on the way up to Doublecreek with all the information she'd gotten from reading, they stopped to talk to a woman, and she was spitting something red. And after exchanging some greetings and explaining they were on their way home, they pulled away and my mother couldn't wait to speak to my father about her. She said, "That woman has cancer of the mouth." And Joe said, "No, she don't have cancer of the mouth; she's chewing tobacco." My mother couldn't fathom that – that a woman would be chewin' tobacco. But it happened a lot in the mountains, I

Martha and Susie Mahler with my grandparents in New York.

suppose for lack of something else to do.

~~~

My mother was a writer. She wrote a column for many, many years for the local newspaper. It was called A Personal View, and she wrote one every week and wrote some in-between in case she wasn't able to write for one reason or another. Everyone in the county knew who she was; she was that blind lady that wrote so well.

One of the great stories she told was about someone in a passage from "Pilgrim's Progress," which besides the Bible was the most read book in early America. Here's the story my mother told. She was in the hospital for 119 days at one stretch, and when she got out she wrote this story:

She said that this man was going up this huge mountain and he was carrying a cross, and it was more than he could carry, and he was dragging it along, struggling, begrudging God for making him carry this cross up this mountain, how tough it was, how impossible it was, how he knew he wadn't goin to make it, and he struggled and he struggled and he struggled, and, eventually, he made it to the top of the mountain. And he relaxed a little bit, he looked around, and he saw all these other folks up there and all of 'em had crosses too. And he began to notice that of all the crosses they were dragging, his was the smallest one of all. This is the story my mother told the week she was out of the hospital.

~~~

My mother told me this story many years ago, when I was just a small boy. I believed then it was a true story, and I still believe today it may be a true story. So I'll tell it like she told it.

Once upon a time there was a bird. The bird was born in the early spring, and had a fantastic summer, and when it started to cool down it was just great up there on the Ohio, where the bird was living. As the days moved along, the bird knew that it was getting a little cooler and a little cooler, and it was so comfortable and there were so many things to eat, all the fields were full of bird feed, and all the birds living there were having the greatest time.

Then one day the bird came in late one afternoon and noticed the whole family was packin' up all their stuff and gettin' ready to leave. So he asked 'em, "Where are yall goin'?" And they said, "Well, we're goin' south for the winter." And he said, "Why would you go south and leave all this great food? It's just now getting cool enough at night to sleep." And they said, "Well, anytime any bird stayed up here when we get the urge to go south, he isn't here when we come back next spring." And he said, "Why is that?" And a wise old bird said, "Well, we don't know. We sometimes see their bones, but we don't know what happened to 'em. But it's a pretty good guess they're not alive when we get back up here. So pack up your stuff and let's go."

But the young bird resisted. He said, "I'm not gonna go. I'm gonna stay here and next year I'll be able to tell you what went on during the winter." So they all gave him a big hug and proceeded to get their crew together and head south.

So the young bird was by himself and a little bit lonely, but it was a wonderful fall and there was plenty of food and it was a great time to be alive. But he did notice it was getting cooler and cooler, and sometimes in the evening it was just about cold. So he decided that what happened was birds got colder and colder and colder and froze to death during the winter. And he was so proud that he figured out what the plight was, that basically he would freeze to death. So he said, "I figured it out just in time. I'm gonna get packed up and leave in the morning."

So the next morning he gets all packed up, and he's flying along south and he's doin' pretty good; then he begins to notice that his wings are kinda icin' up a little bit. So he thinks,"If I can just make it to Chattanooga, everything will be okay, and then I can go on south." So he's flying over the Lipps farm, and all of a sudden he lost all sense of feeling in his wings, and he slowly began losing altitude, and all at once he hit the ground. And he said to himself, "I'm gonna die here in the snow, and they're gonna come back in the spring, and I'm gonna be dead and gone and they won't know what happened to me. Oh, woe is me."

And then he heard this thunderous, thunderous noise, and he looked down across the field and saw this big ol' Holstein cow walking toward him, and he thought, "Oh my goodness, I'm gonna be killed by a Holstein cow steppin' on me. I'm a bird; I'm supposed to be in the air. A cow's not supposed to be steppin' on me." Nevertheless, here comes a big cow.

So the cow comes up to where the bird is layin' and the

cow starts to go to the bathroom and just covers the bird up in manure. So he kinda shook his head out of it, and he noticed the manure was hot, and then he noticed that his body was startin' to heat up, and at some point he decided he could fly again. And he was such a happy bird that he began to sing. He began to sing because he thought he could make it down south and come back next spring. And his singing became so loud that a mean and hungry cat who hadn't had anything to eat since the snow fell four days ago heard the bird singing somewhere. So the cat looked around and saw where the bird was, and he got up and took one big leap at the bird, and he swallowed him in one big bite. The bird was gone.

There were three important morals to this story that my mother told me: The first one is, everybody who poops on you isn't necessarily your enemy. On the other hand, everybody who poops on you isn't necessarily your friend. But if you're gonna waller around in poop, keep your doggone mouth shut.

~~~

My mother once told about and wrote a story from the great Kentucky writer Jesse Stuart who wrote a book called "Taps for Private Tussie." This guy was injured during WWII, and the Army made a determination that he could not make it home on his own. So instead of sending somebody with him or anything, they just put a freight tag on him. They actually pinned a freight tag to his clothes, so he became freight coming back to a rural area. So when the local constabulary found out one of their own was coming home with a freight tag, they assumed he was in a casket, that he was dead. So they gave his parents the $10,000 insurance, and they went up and rented the town mansion which was vacant at the time, and had as many as 40 people lined up to go to the newfangled bathroom that was in it.

It was a bestseller, and on coming to Kentucky, my mother read "Taps for Private Tussie" as an example to find out what was happenin' where she was goin'. So try to imagine someone coming from New York City to the mountains of East Kentucky and reading "Taps for Private Tussiey" as an example of what she might expect. It took a lot of bravery to leave New York and come to somewhere where there was not a sidewalk in sight.

~~~

My mother was a great writer. She wrote for many, many years for our award-winning weekly newspaper, the Sentinel Echo of London, Kentucky. At some point her columns were in many papers in eastern Kentucky. The name of her column was A Personal View, and she wrote about everything under the sun. She'd never been to a football game but she wrote about football during the tournaments. She explained to the people of Laurel County, Kentucky, why Ireland had no snakes. She was one of the most read people in the county.

When she passed away, there were two front-page articles

about her career, and the person who wrote those articles was just as talented a writer as she was. He wrote about her blindness and her courage and her integrity to stick to the story.

She typed her own columns on her Braille typewriter, and Joe took 'em up to the editors at the Sentinel Echo a few blocks away. When she was able to see, she read a book a day, and nobody could ask a question she didn't have the answer to. She answered all the questions on "Truth or Consequences." Her goal was to get on one of those game shows where they ask you questions; she never did, but she would have undoubtedly won the big prize if she had. She was very well read, and she was a fantastic writer.

I, on the other hand, thought I might be a writer myself, even though I can't spell, my grammatical mistakes are plentiful, and if I did not have a wonderful editor on this particular book, I could not do it. I determined this: My mother was a writer; I am not a writer. But I have been a storyteller most of my life. My grandfather was a storyteller, my father was a storyteller, and I'm a storyteller. We have applied poetic license as far as we could spread it. If you've been around me for very long, you have heard me say, "That reminds me of a story."

Susie Lipps used a Braille typewriter to prepare her columns for the Sentinel Echo.

~~~

When my friend Lloyd and I were travelin' up and down I-75 trying to make a livin', we would often stop by my mother and dad's house and when we were in the mountains, we'd stop by his mother and dad's house. And when we'd start to leave my mother would always say to us, "I can give you boys a hundred dollar bill, or I can give you boys a big hug, whichever one you want." So we would look at each other, and we'd say, "We'll take a big hug." So my mother would give us each a big hug.

And we'd get out and get a few miles from my parents' home and we'd say, "What was we thinkin'? We don't have ten dollars together, and she was gonna give us two hundred dollars, and we didn't take it. What is wrong with us?"

When she passed away I understand she had a bunch of hundred dollar bills in her wheelchair.

JOE

My father helped the whole community of Possum Trot at one time or another. He had three or four things that he did that really worked out. One, he went to an agricultural school after he got out of the Army. He and three or four of his friends went down to Lily High School where they learned how to farm. They were natural farmers but they didn't know some of the scientific methods that had been developed after World War II. My father was lucky enough to be in those classes, and I think he may have been paid to be in those classes – one of the good government things that has been done.

Anyway, most people put out tobacco, and as a cover crop they put rye grass, which is a big, heavy grass that grew waist high, and you ploughed it under, and it provided moisture for the rest of the year for the tobacco to mature in. But my father found out that turnips and turnip greens are just as good as rye grass so he planted a couple acres of turnips and turnip greens. We didn't eat turnips or turnip greens, for some unknown reason, 'cuz we love 'em now, but anybody in the community – some even came from 25 miles away – could come and pick all the greens they wanted and take 'em home with 'em – we gave 'em away.

In the same vein, Joe would get a 100-pound bag of planting potatoes and he would get all the eyes out, and us boys would plant those potatoes – seemed like an acre or so of 'em – and in the fall when the potatoes were done growin' , we'd take a small tractor that we had and plough one time down the middle of the row and whatever came up we'd go behind the tractor and pick up and put 'em in the barn to serve us during the winter. But there was only a small portion of the potatoes that you could plough up like that. So anybody that wanted to could come and bring a hoe and dig up what was left of those potatoes, so there was always somebody there diggin' up potatoes. We just gave 'em to 'em, no charge or anything for 'em.

And when anybody needed anything done with cattle, we had all the equipment to work with the cattle, everybody's cattle. We did all the castrations in the community, we did all the de-horning; anytime a calf or a cow was sick we went and got the proper medicine and gave it to the cow.

So my father was up on farming. We had the best farm in the community, we grew the most tobacco per acre, and we grew the most hay per acre, and from time to time he would insult one of our neighbors by asking if he could put some watermelons on his property. Our farmland was too rich to grow watermelons but his was just right. So my father was an excellent farmer.

~~~

There was a time when there was a big stir: Was there oil in the hills of Possum Trot? There was a group of investors – doctors and lawyers – and they drove a big ol' black Cadillac, and they came into town and determined that Joe was the number one, most respected citizen in Possum Trot. So they drove straight to our house, and they asked him how much a day he would take to drive them around to the neighbors' houses and talk to all the people about buying the oil rights and the opportunities there was in maybe coal or oil on the property they owned. So Joe put on his cleanest pair of overalls, and he decided there was oil in them thar hills, and he was gonna have everybody get part of it.

So they went house to house, and he negotiated the deal with each farmer, usually around two or three dollars an acre for lease, which was never gonna be worth anything because there wasn't any coal and there wasn't any oil there. So everybody got a little bit of money outta the deal; the larger the farm the more money they got, but everybody got some benefit from it. It's been fifty-some years now, and nobody ever discovered oil or coal near where Joe helped these people make a few dollars. He did not look like an oil man, but he was pretty savvy, so he rode around for about six months in a big black Cadillac, and he made a few hundred dollars a week helping people decide whether to lease the mineral rights to their land for the oil that might be on it.

~~~

An ongoing argument for about fifty years was is the Earth flat. Joe insisted the Earth was flat, and I spent a good portion of my life trying to convince him that it wadn't flat. We raised tobacco, and there was a time during the wintertime when it was very cold during the holidays and on weekends we graded tobacco; we took the tobacco and put it in different grades, and we talked about a lot of different stuff, and one of the issues I had with Joe was is the Earth flat. He believed it was, and I didn't think so. And so we talked about that a lot. We talked about it to the point he told me to shut up and not discuss it anymore.

So I would say, "If the Earth is flat, what happens when you get to the edge of it? You know, it can't go on forever. Why don't your car go runnin' over the edge, you know?" And he said, "Well, there's some kind of power that keeps that from happenin'; I can't put my finger on it, don't know exactly what it is, but you can't run over the edge of the Earth.

Now he attributed the Earth is flat theory to a verse in the Bible that said the four horsemen of the Apocalypse stood on the four corners of the Earth or something like that, so obviously the Earth had to be flat if you had to have corners. So I would take a piece of paper and draw a circle and then I would draw a square over top of it, and I would say, "See, that is what they're talking about; this is a corner; it can be square there," He didn't agree, you know?

I knew he had been down to the ocean when he was in the Army, to New York and New Jersey, so I said, "Have you ever walked down to the beach and seen the water rise up in front of you, thus showing the curvature of the Earth?" And he'd say, "I've seen that, I've seen that, but that's just the tide comin in, that's all that is."

So we would banter back and forth for hours on this Earth is flat thing, and there are people who thought that Joe eventually decided that the Earth wadn't flat, but he never admitted it to me; he continued to say in my presence that the Earth is flat. But my brothers thought he only did that to irritate me. What they didn't know is I enjoyed the banter and it wadn't irritatin' me at all. I always thought he believed what he was sayin', that the Earth is flat. And he not only believed it, but many of his friends believed it, too.

~~~

The Beach Boys at Cumberland Falls State Park: Joe, Ab, Ralph and Ray.

There was a time I was living by my wits, and I got involved in buying these returns from General Foods up in New Jersey. Instead of dumping the tractor trailer loads and payin' to get rid of 'em, I made a deal to send 'em to Lexington to me, and I would figure a way to get rid of 'em. I was not paying anything for the tractor trailer loads of Geritol, Tylenol, Menon shaving lotion – things they were returnin' off their shelves when a place went bankrupt or whatever, so I had warehouses full of that stuff. So I took Joe down some Tylenol. I took him like twenty bottles and told him to share it with his friends, you know – these were bottles of 100. So when we had the big Tylenol scare, Joe called me up, and he said, "Ray, I need some more of that Tyl-nol." And I said, "What do you need more Tylenol for?" He said, "Well, I had eight bottles of that Tyl-nol, and I took it across the street to the convenient mart, and they gave me eleven dollars apiece back for those eight bottles," or whatever he took over there. He said, "I could use a bunch more of it." I told him, "I don't have any more Tylenol, Joe. I gave it away or sold it," and I said, "That's a very enterprising thing you done here." Had he had a couple hundred bottles, we could've gone to Las Vegas and gambled with it or something. It was very valuable stuff for a while.

~~~

About 30 years ago, I had a young lady working for me who was friends with a person who taught at Draughons Junior College in Knoxville. And they were lookin' for someone to do the commencement speech, and, by chance, they asked me if I would do this; and in fact, they offered to pay me if I would do this twenty-minute speech, and the subject was, "How have things changed in your lifetime?" So I knew six months in advance about having to do this speech, so I started to think about how I would respond. I tried to write it several times, and I was not having a whole lot of luck coming up with something I was satisfied with that would be a good talk and something I know something about.

So anyway, I had my father down for the week, and it was Sunday afternoon, and we were at S&S Cafeteria gettin' some lunch, and I asked Joe, I said, "Joe, since you were young, what's the most significant change that's been made in your life?" He was about 75 years old at the time, you know.

So he said, "Well, you know," he said, "just what we're doing here." I said, "What do you mean? We're just out to eat." He said, "That's the point. That's the point. We used to eat at home and go out to use the bathroom, and now we use the bathroom at home and go out to eat." I thought this was unequivocal proof that there has been change in our lives.

~~~

After my mother passed away, about once a month I would bring my father from London down to Knoxville, where I lived, and he would stay three or four days, and we always had a good time. We'd go out to eat together, and he'd get up early, and I'd have to go find him; he'd be in one of the rooms, sittin' in a chair, chewin' his tobacco, just relaxin'. At that time we owned a restaurant, and we'd go down to the restaurant, where he would hang out the whole day and look at people and eat with the girls that worked down there, and he enjoyed it.

So he would come down and spend three or four days with me, and I always tried to do something for him, and on this particular visit he needed a new pair of shoes. So we went to several shoe stores before we found a pair that fit him good and looked nice, that was light and easy to get on – just a really perfect pair of shoes for him. They cost about forty dollars, so I sprung for the forty dollars and bought him this nice pair of shoes.

So a few days later, I was up in London and we were over at his house, and my brother Ralph walked in, and I looked down at his shoes, and I said, "Those are great lookin' shoes; I just bought Joe a pair of those." And he said, "That's who I got 'em from; I got 'em from Joe."

And I said, "What do you mean you got 'em from Joe?" And he said, "He sold 'em to me yesterday." And I said, "What do you mean he sold 'em to you?" He said, "Well, he sold 'em to me for twenty bucks."

I didn't find humor in that at all, but after a while I decided that is a funny story. He took the shoes that I'd bought him for forty dollars, and he sold 'em to Ralph for twenty dollars, and he made a profit of twenty bucks on the shoes.

~~~

There was a time when Joe was supposed to go a block or two from his house and have his blood pressure taken once a week. And I was always on him to make sure that happened.

On one of my trips into London to see these guys, the Spit

'n Whittle Club, we were sittin' there on a summer day during the week in Joe's living room, and Orb Moseley gets up outta his chair and goes over to my mother's desk, opens up the desk, takes out a shoestring. And I watched very intently what he was doin', you know.

So he takes the shoestring over to Joe's chair, and he ties the shoestring around Joe's arm above his elbow and he puts his thumb in the crook of his elbow, turns his head sideways like he's listenin', like somebody takin' blood pressure with the blood pressure machine, you know. And he does that for a little bit, and he says, "Joe, your blood pressure's OK for today."

So I was settin' there stewin', you know. I knew that Joe was supposed to go and get his blood pressure taken by the doctor, and here he was lettin' this guy take his blood pressure with a shoestring. And I was thinkin', "How dumb can these guys get," you know.

My Aunt Martha was there. She came and spent a month with our family some summers, and after my mother died, she continued to do that, and she was there with the Spit n Whittle Club that mornin', and my Aunt Martha had a good education from a New York college, and she said, "Orb, can you take mine?"

Well, that put me over the top there, you know. So I said, "Martha, Joe, outside." So we go out on the porch, and I say, "What are you people doin'? You know that guy can't take blood pressure with a shoestring." And I said, "Joe, you know you're supposed to be up there at the doctor's office gettin' your blood pressure checked." And Joe said, "Of COURSE I go get my blood pressure checked like I'm supposed to. You don't think I think that guy can take my blood pressure, do you? I know he can't take it, but he wants to do that, and there's no harm in it to me, so I let him do it."

And I turned around to Martha, and I said, "Martha, what's with you?" you know. And she said, "Well, he'd been takin' Joe's blood pressure so I thought he could take mine too, you know?"

~~~

Joe Lipps

For over seventeen years, Joe had to go to Lexington to the VA Hospital to have water cysts checked that were on his kidneys. And that duty fell to me because I was the only one of the three boys who didn't have a job, so to speak. I worked for myself so therefore I didn't have a job, so I had time to do this. My brothers had jobs that they had to go to and punch a clock, I guess, so it fell to me to take him to Lexington each month to have this test.

A day at the hospital was an exciting day for the older person, and each of the elder people sitting in a row had a younger person, a relative, that had brought them to the VA Hospital. And so the older people were getting paid sixty, seventy dollars a day to buy food and pay for gas, none of which they ever shared, I'm pretty sure, with the younger people bringing 'em.

It was a big day for Joe — he often found someone he knew from Clay County – and it was a long day for me. I would leave my house at five o'clock in the morning and I would get to Joe's house around seven o'clock and then whether the door was locked, whether the gas was on, we'd go through those routines and we would get to Lexington about nine o'clock.

And you didn't dare let Joe out of the car at the door. If you parked a mile away you had to take him with you. Because if you left him at the door he'd get himself checked into the hospital one way or another and it'd take a couple weeks to get him out. That's another reason my brothers didn't handle this job because he'd end up in the hospital when they took him. And they would be late getting there; there were a lot of reasons that I did this job. As I look back on it, it was a great time to ride and talk and hear some of these stories.

As I said, at the hospital it was an old person and a young person, an old person and a young person, and the old person was wide-eyed and fully alert, looking to see someone he knew, and the young person was trying to catch a wink, and there were all kinds of things goin' on to disturb you from sleeping.

One of the days we went – I've always called it the Thermometer Day – there was a new doctor in town, and Joe was seeing him about something, and this doctor sits Joe down in the hallway. Not in a room, but in the hallway where everybody else was sittin', you know. And he puts a thermometer in Joe's mouth, and then he proceeds to go to lunch and forgets about Joe.

So Joe's sittin there in the hallway with a thermometer in his mouth, it was glass, and I thought he would crunch down on it and break it eventually, so I tried to talk him into giving up the thermometer before the doctor got back. I tried to convince him that the doctor had left town, you know, and he should take this thermometer out of his mouth before he had an accident with it.

Well, he refused to do that. He said the doctor put it in there, and the doctor would be back to check it anytime. So

47

we sat there for about an hour and 20 minutes, and finally the doctor came in, and I did not just casually mention that my father had had this thermometer in his mouth for almost an hour and a half. And of course the doctor apologized profusely and admitted he had forgotten him.

So that afternoon on the way home, Joe lectured me, he said, "You should never have jumped on that doctor. He was just doin' his job. And you jumped on him like he did something drastic. I was not gonna bite that thermometer; it wasn't dangerous, and I didn't mind a bit waitin' for him to get back from lunch to take that thermometer out of my mouth." So he chewed me pretty good about it, and I learned that doctors don't make mistakes. Sons and daughters make mistakes, but doctors don't.

~~~

Some of the best stories about Joe took place on our rides to Lexington, Kentucky. For many years I would come up and get Joe and take him to the VA Hospital to be checked out for one reason or another.

The reason my brothers couldn't take him is they had jobs that they had to go to, and everybody always thought I was unemployed because I didn't have a job working for somebody else. We worked for ourselves, Lloyd Abdoo and I did, and my mother and my dad always thought that we needed to get a job, you know. So I was given the job of taking Joe to Lexington when he had to go.

One of the first problems with taking Joe to Lexington is you had to be on time. He had no tolerance for people who were gonna be late picking him up and taking him anywhere. And so over the years I tried never to be late; I think I was late one time; there was a wreck on the interstate, and I was a few minutes late getting' there. It seemed like a few minutes tortured him, you know; he wanted to be on time. My brothers didn't quite understand that. So it fell to me to take him to Lexington.

One of the things he did to my brothers when they took him to Lexington was they'd get about twenty miles from home, and he'd say, "Did I turn off the gas?" Or "Did I lock the door?" He wouldn't let up until you went back and checked it, you know.

So whenever I picked him up, I had this routine; I'd go in and watch him turn the gas off, and about two minutes later I'd say, "I don't think we turned the gas off," and he'd say, "Yeah we did; we just did it," and I'd say, "I don't think so." I would talk him into going back and checkin' the gas again. And he'd say, "I TOLD you we turned it off. You see, it's off!" And I'd wait about two or three minutes and say, "Did we turn off the gas?" and he'd get kind of disturbed with me and he'd say, "We turned off the gas, Ray! You've asked me that three or four times now; the gas is off!" I would say OK.

And then we'd go out and we'd lock the door, and I'd shake the door till the glass about fell out of it, you know, and he'd say, "Don't shake that door like that; it's locked," and so I'd wait a little bit, and then I'd shake the door again. I'd say, "I don't know if it's locked or not, Joe." And he'd say, "It's locked, it's locked!"

So we would get up the road fifteen or twenty miles, and he'd say, "Did I turn off the gas?" I'd say, "Sure you did, Joe, we almost had a fistfight about it." And he'd say, "Yeah, that's right, we did." And we'd go a little ways farther, and he'd say, "Did we lock the door?" and I'd say, "Yes, Joe, we locked the door; we almost had a fistfight about that," and he'd say, "I guess I remember that."

And when you got up to the VA you didn't dare let him out of the car because he'd go in and they'd check him in and he'd be in there two weeks before we'd get him back out. So if there was six inches of snow in the road or if it was pouring down rain, you had to take him to the place where you parked; you couldn't let him out early, and so many of my favorite stories are stories I heard while traveling with Joe.

~~~

On one of these monthly trips to the VA Hospital we did what had become a tradition on these excursions to Lexington, Kentucky. My brothers would try to get away from their jobs, and we would all go over to the Kentucky Fried Chicken on Nicholasville Road where we would eat lunch before we went home.

Now Joe never felt any obligation to pay for lunch, even though I'd driven my car and spent my day; my brothers and I always bought him lunch and he took the seventy-nine dollars the VA gave him home with him. And we didn't resent that; my mother would have reminded us that they did raise us and send us to college. And they did SOME of that raisin' and sendin' to college, but we took care of a good portion of it ourselves. One of the most admirable things we accomplished was paying for our college along with Cumberland College helping us get through that.

Joe never felt any obligation to pay for our lunch, and he questioned some of the things that we might participate in. For instance, we were there one day having Kentucky Fried Chicken, and Joe thought we were flirting with the waitresses. We were young guys at the time, and we knew we were just having a pleasant conversation, but Joe thought there should be some kind of an explanation made before we left there about the behavior of his three sons.

So as we were leaving here's what he said. He walked up to the manager of the place, and he said, "I would like to apologize for my sons, but I will tell you this: They do not live at home anymore." That was his way of saying he had no more control over our actions and he absolved himself of all responsibility for what we might do then and in the future.

~~~

Joe's house was approximately two blocks from the courthouse, and the Spit and Whittle Club moved down to his house after my mother passed away. I would visit them on many occasions, and I always brought up some subject that resulted in entertaining comments on their part. My brothers were also there sometimes, and my brother Abner especially could not stand all the BS these guys came up with, and I promoted it every opportunity I got.

I came up there one day, and I walked in the house, and I said, "Folks, I just bought me a ticket to go up to the moon. It cost me $40,000, and I can take somebody with me, and they bought them a Kentucky Fried Chicken up there, you know, and we can go up and have a chicken dinner and come on back before dark. Anybody wanna do that?" And, of course, there was no volunteers to go to the moon, but these were the kinds of topics that we covered.

I would come to London every couple of weeks on Tuesday afternoon to visit the Spit N Whittle Club. The Spit N Whittle Club was a group of men who originally were up at the courthouse on a daily basis, and they spent their time whittling on cedar sticks to see how thin they could cut 'em till they had a big pile of shavings.

It was on an inclement day that Ab and I met at Joe's house about the same time, and all of these folks was there, watching TV, of course. At the beginning of our stay there that day Mary Bradley, who was married to George Bradley, who was one of our great friends out on the farm

52

– he was a person who worked in Detroit and made a substantial amount of money and he had a nice little farm down below our farm, and we did a fair amount of work for him. George Bradley was one of those great people you meet in life who know a lot about a lot of things, and as a young fella growing up who was destined to go to college and start a business, I was interested in George Bradley.

Now his wife Mary, uh, she was different. She talked a lot, and you couldn't hardly get away from her, you know. She was starved for someone to talk about the day's events with, and it was on one of these days when we were there in London, Mary Bradley called up and asked to talk to me; she pretty much knew what days I'd be there.

So Mary and I are on the phone, and Ab, he needs to make a phone call; this was a few years before cell phones. So here we are in the living room; I'm talking to Mary Bradley, and there's an extension phone off of the phone I was on in the bedroom. And of course Orb Mosely was there, and Abner kept saying to me, "Ray, get off the phone. I need to make a very important phone call." And Orb would chime in and say, "Yeah, Ab, go in the bedroom and use that phone."

Instead of explaining to Orb that those phones were on the same line, he would just get madder and madder and madder. So he would come in the living room and give me a threatening look like "Get off the damn phone; I've got to make this phone call." And every time he would do this,

I'd say, "Well, Orb told you; go in the bedroom and make your call in there."

He was getting madder and madder and madder, and Mary Bradley, of course, didn't have a clue what was going on. And the Spit N Whittle Club didn't have a clue; it was just a thing between Ab and I, where I acted like I didn't know the other phone was connected, just like folks up there thought they weren't connected to each other. That happened many times when we were there, Ab and I together, to distract ourselves from the crazy conversations going on around us.

~~~

There was a time the Spit N Whittle Club came down to Joe's house to watch "Bonanza" four times and "The Virginian" five times and "Wagon Train" a coupla times a day, and the black-and-white TV they always watched went kaput.

So he called me to see if I could find him a TV, and I went lookin' around Knoxville to see if I could find a large screen, black-and-white TV. After a time, I decided there wasn't such an animal; you could get a small one, but they didn't make a large one.

So I told Joe, I said, "Joe, I don't think I can find a black-and-white TV; I can get you a color one." He said, "Well, I don't really want a color one." I said, "Well, give it a try."

So I brought a color TV to the house, and everybody took a vote on how to handle the situation. They decided that color TV causes cancer, and the way to get around it was to turn all the color off of it.

So for the rest of their lives, they watched a TV with a screen that was green. And, as far as I know, none of 'em died from cancer. So avoiding color TV saved their lives, and none of 'em got cancer. This is a little known fact: Color TV causes cancer. Black-and-white TV does not cause cancer. And evidently, green TV doesn't cause cancer either.

~~~

Every couple o' weeks I would come up and Ab would come down and Ralph would come over, and we'd sit and listen and see what's goin' on with those folks. And so I always tried to get 'em stirred up, and it always disturbed Abner especially that he wasn't fixed to put up with the

craziness of these guys, so I'd come in and say somethin' like, "Hey, guys, what you all think about AIDS? It's a dreaded disease, idn't it?" Orb said, "No, it's not a disease," And I'd say, "It isn't? I thought it was a disease." And he say, "No, it's not a disease; you acquire it." And I said, "How do you acquire it?" He said, "Worry."

I said, "I think you might have something there. I think you might have something. But how do you account for about 95 percent of the people having it are homosexual?" He said, "Well, Ray," he said, "they worry more than anybody."

~~~

There was a time in the last few days of Joe's life that Lloyd Abdoo and I went to see him at three o'clock in the morning. They let us in, and we talked to him, and then we went our separate ways; Lloyd went back to where he lived, and I drove back to Knoxville.

And as I came in my house the phone was ringing; it was about 6:30. This young doctor was on the phone, and she asked me, she said, "Can you come to Lexington?" I said, "I just left Lexington this morning. I just got home. What's wrong?"

And she said, "You need to come and talk to your father," and I said, "Put him on the phone. I'll talk to him right now." She said, "He won't talk on the phone." I said, "Okay, can you tell me what's goin' on?" and she said, "He has threatened to blow up the place. And he has threatened to shoot some people."

And I said, "Have you all issued him a bomb?" She said, "You think this is funny?" I said, "Well, no. I have to admit there's some humor in it, because he doesn't have a bomb and unless you all issued him one he's not goin' to blow up the place. And I've got all his pistols so we know he's not gonna shoot anybody. So it's not a big threat that he's making if he is making that kind of threat." She said, "Well, can you come up here?" And I said, "Well, I guess I could." So I changed clothes and headed back to Lexington.

Well, I drove and I wondered what I would say to him when I got there, you know. And I got there and I had some candy bars. He and his roommate could not eat chocolate, but they could eat Zero bars, which had white chocolate on 'em. So I always brought 'em a couple each whenever I went up to visit, so I gave 'em their candy bars, and they're sittin' there eatin' their candy bars, and I asked Joe, I said, "Uh, anything exciting happen this morning, Joe?" He said, "Not that I know of."

I said, "You been involved in some kind of problem up here?" and he said, "Well, I don't think so." And I said, "Did you tell some people you were gonna blow up the place?" He said, "Well, I don't remember doing that."

So before I came in the room I was talking to this nurse, and she said that he had threatened her. So she came into the room about that time, and I pointed over toward the nurse, and I said, "Did you tell this lady right here that you were gonna do her some kind of harm?" And he said, "I wadn't serious."

I found great humor in that, but nobody up there found much humor in it.

I told Joe, I said, "Joe, you can't be threatenin' to blow up the place, and you can't be threatenin' to kill people. You just have to cool it a little bit." And that was the conversation for the day.

~~~

My dad was a true character, in that true characters never realize that they're characters.

In the last few days of Joe's life he was coming and going as far as his mentality there, and my brothers didn't feel like you could have a conversation with him because he was out of his head. And so I told them that I'd experienced talking to people out of their heads in Possum Trot all my life, so what was wrong with talking to Joe, you know?

So I asked him, I said, "Can I bring you some pineapple upside down cake?", which was one of his favorites, and he said no, he didn't want upside down cake, and I said, "Well, how about banana pudding?" He said, "No, I don't want no banana pudding." So I said, "What about I go out and get you some tobacco," — he chewed tobacco all his life — he said, "No, I'm not gonna chew tobacco anymore."

I said, "I know what I'll do. I'll go get a VCR and bring some John Wayne movies up here for you." He said, "I'm not gonna hang out with John Wayne no more."

And I said, "My goodness, that's a major statement you made there 'cuz you loved John Wayne all your life." And he said, "I'm not hanging out with him no more," and I said, "Well, can you tell me why?"

And he said, "You know that locust post down there behind the outhouse back at the farm?" and I said, "Yes, I know that post." He said, "I was down there with John Wayne the other day, and I went down and cut a little smooth place on the post and I put a cross on it, and I stepped back about 30 feet with my flat-barrel Haroldson Richardson .22 pistol, and I put a bullet right in the center, right in the center of the cross. And I handed the pistol to John Wayne, and he aimed carefully, and he shot, and he missed the whole damn post. So I'm not hanging out with him anymore."

So I told Joe, I said, "You know, I think I know what happened, and I'm gonna be down there in the next couple of days, and I'm goin' by that post, and I'm gonna dig out the bullets, and HIS bullet is gonna be right in behind yours."

So Joe thought about that a minute, and he said, "Ray, you're full of crap," letting us know that he wasn't entirely out of his head.

TEACHERS

Mr. Bentley was the principal of Bush High School for many, many, many years, and I was the recipient of his huge dedication to the students of Bush High School under his tenure. He never missed a day of school for a personal reason for better than fifty years. I equate this to walking on the moon.

He was a very staunch man. When one of the teachers sent you to see him, you knew you were going to the principal's office, and you knew it was not going to be a happy affair. But you also knew he would do what was fair. Sometimes it was hard to stomach, but he was a fair man. He had a keen sense of humor, and he was intelligent, and we were lucky to have a man such as him there.

Mr. Bentley was a gardener, and he came up with this idea about the chestnut trees that were killed in a blight in the

1940s or earlier, and so there were no chestnut trees anywhere in eastern Kentucky. And he set upon a Johnny Appleseed journey to replenish the wonderful chestnut trees in eastern Kentucky. And he had the Key Club and other clubs and almost everybody in high school plant some 6,500 chestnut trees in Laurel County. And they're still there. What a tribute to what a man.

I could name a whole bunch of teachers we were lucky to have: Miss Evans; Mr. Bentley's wife was the librarian, and she was fantastic; Bobby Tuttle; Wayne Bowling; Mr. Baker; Mr. Parrott; Mrs. Parrott; Joe Tom Gregory; Larry Stamper; Mr. Peters; Mr. Garland; and Mr. Hill. They were all wonderful teachers; every single one of them was great, and I was influenced by most of them in one way or another, and I loved them all.

~~~

Bush High School

How about a Joe Tom Gregory story? Joe Tom was the basketball coach and the track coach and the baseball coach at Bush High School. He was a rough, gruff coach, and most of us liked him; I had a lifelong relationship with my friend and coach Joe Tom Gregory. There are not many people who could hang with Joe Tom; I was one of the few people who could put up with him more than a few hours. Every year for many years we went down to Florida where he had a small orchard, and we would pick a pickup truck bed full of oranges, and we'd bring 'em back and put 'em in boxes and set 'em on people's porches. It was our good deed for the year, and a lot of people never knew who set 'em on the porch.

There was a time when we stayed one night with his cousin in Tallahassee on the Panhandle, and as we were leaving the next morning we had to go down a ways from his house and there was a crossroads, and you turned right and in about three seconds you were on the interstate heading back toward London, Kentucky. So Joe Tom traded for this small Corvair station wagon, and it had such a short wheel base he couldn't back it up. He hitched it to the back of his pickup truck and we were takin' it home. So when he got down to this place where he should've turned right, he turned left. And I said, "Coach, you turned the wrong way." And he said, "No, I didn't. What makes you so smart? You think I can't drive?" you know. And I said, "Well, I know you can drive; you're driving right now. But you're going the wrong way." We argued about that until I looked over to my right, and there was the house we spent the night in; he'd come full-circle around the subdivision and we were passing where we first started. I said, "You recognize that house over there?" and he said, "Yeah, I guess I turned the wrong way," so we go down to this stop sign where we should've turned right, and he turns left again. So I was bugging him; I said, "You dummy, you turned the wrong way again," and this time, it was like, "I'll throw your ass out of the truck if you don't shut up," and we argued until we got around to the house we spent the night in, and I said, "You recognize that house?" He said, "How'd I do that? I got down there and turned the wrong way twice." So we come up on the intersection again, and he says to me, "You're so smart; which way do we turn?" And I said, "Left." He gets about fifty feet, and he realizes I told him wrong, and he gets so mad at me. He threatens to throw me out of the truck; he threatens to report me to my parents, and we didn't speak a lot on the trip home. He stayed mad at me for a week or two. He finally got over it.

~~~

Joe Tom Gregory and his wife Mary Gregory loved me and Lloyd and Kenny. They loved to see us, and I remember one time Lloyd was driving a two-ton truck, and I was driving a van, and I had a Cadillac, which Kenny was driving. We were coming from Knoxville to Pikeville, and we get over to the exit where my high school coach lived, so we decided we'd go over there and ask Mary to make us some fried apples and some scrambled eggs. There was nothing else open to get something to eat, so we went on over to my coach's house and we got 'em out of bed, and he was glad to see us. It didn't matter what time we showed up, Joe Tom and Mary were always glad to see us.

But I'm getting ahead of myself. We were sittin' on the side of the road trying to determine if we were going to the coach's house or not, and we tried to discuss it with Kenny, and he was asleep in the Cadillac. The car was running, and we were on the side of the interstate, and I couldn't get into my car. He had locked the doors and he had the key. So we beat on the doors and we beat on the windows, we hollered, we screamed, we shook the car, we bounced on it. He wouldn't wake up. We were there like an hour, and when we finally got him awake we went over to Joe Tom and Mary's and asked 'em to fix us some eggs, which they were so gracious to do.

~~~

Wayne Bowling was my biology teacher. Now biology wasn't my favorite course, but there was a time when I was in class with a lot of other people who shouldn't have been there, and we were studying the innards of a frog, for a reason unknown to me. During that study, Mr. Bowling went out of the room for a few minutes, and when he came back there was a lively battle going on with frog innards. We were throwing them at each other.

He surveyed what had gone on in his absence, and he looked back at me and said, "Mr. Lipps, in the hallway, please." So I went out to the hallway, and I knew I was gonna be in deep trouble.

And Mr. Bowling came up to me and he said, "I am surprised that you would be involved in this kind of endeavor. You're here to get an education. If you were one of these people" – he mentioned two or three names – "I would probably not say much about it. But you're going somewhere in the future, and you're going to accomplish great things. So I'm surprised to see you involved in this kind of deal.

"So I'm gonna ask you never to do this sort of thing again, and I'm gonna forget about any kind of punishment for you. You remember as you go through life that this was the place that said, 'Go out and do good.'"

~~~

Mr. Sasser was the vice principal of Bush High School when I attended there, 1962-66. Mr. Sasser only taught one course. This course was Advanced Chemistry. There was nobody in that course who should've been there. My brother Ralph and I were two of the people who took that course, and Ralph was more apt to be there and be successful than I was. But as it turned out, neither he nor I missed a question in that course, and Mr. Sasser was very partial to us.

Mr. Sasser was the sort of man we don't have many of anymore. He was a great teacher, he was a great principal of a kind of unruly high school, and he just did his job fantastically. So when we took the final test, one of the questions on the test was: Define a vacuum.

So I used this example. I will not mention the name, but I said this person's name who was in my class – his head was a vacuum.

When Mr. Sasser read my response, he came over to my desk, and he said, "Well, Mr. Lipps, I guess I'm gonna have to give you this one, but don't do it again." Mr. Sasser was not a man who was very funny, but he found some humor in what I'd said that day, and he immediately knew that I knew what a vacuum was.

CUMBERLAND COLLEGE

Off to College in a Cattle Truck. That's the title of this account of the Lipps boys' lives, and it's a good title. It took a long time to come to it. It seems to be one that everyone enjoys, and it's understandable. Ralph, Ab and I had no other transportation to go to college other than the cattle truck, and when we got there we parked it and went back home on weekends, you know, to work in the tobacco and hay fields to earn enough money to go back to school and pay what we had to pay at Cumberland.

Anyway, I hope it's a catchy title, and I hope it helps people understand how poor we were up in the eastern Kentucky mountains, and how much Cumberland did to help us get an education. "We came in cattle trucks and we left in Cadillacs." We'd like to say that but it wouldn't be true. We came in cattle trucks and we left with an education that allowed most of us to be very successful in life, and we were no different.

Dr. Boswell, Cumberland's president, had a routine where he would go for an hour or so many mornings to play tennis, then he would go home, take a shower and get his clothes on, and then he would walk across campus to his office. And Abner somehow could time that pretty accurately, and he'd be sitting out there in the street, and he'd say, "Get in, Dr. B., ride with me."

So Dr. B. would climb up over the whips and the ropes and the cow manure and the hot sticks and whatever else was there in the cattle truck, and he would climb up over the top of all that stuff, and Ab would take him over to his office. Dr. B. enjoyed doing that, and Abner enjoyed doing it for him, you know. Dr. B. rode in that cattle truck about as much as we did during those four years at Cumberland.

~~~

When we were all young and in college, my younger brother Abner often went to Jellico when he should've been studying. It was on one of these trips that he took several of his friends, and Wayne Vanzant had this Corvair, so like eight of 'em piled into this Corvair to go down to Jellico and have a few beers.

The place they went was on the far side of Jellico, so they had a little ways to go through town to get to the interstate, and goin' through town someone in the car wondered if they could make it back to the interstate drivin' on the sidewalks. They were drivin' up and down steps and around on the sidewalks, you know, to get back to the interstate.

Of course, the police nabbed 'em. There were like seven or eight of 'em in that car, and he takes 'em down to jail, and they were sittin' around in that waiting room.

Now the Jellico police did not want to put anyone from Cumberland in jail, you know, so they tried to work it out. They came in and gave everybody a good look, and there was a basketball player there and several other people that shouldn't have been out, and they were lookin' for someone who had not had as much to drink as the other guys so they could rest assured that if they let that person drive, they could make it home without being killed, you know.

So they decided Abner might've not had as much to drink as some of the other boys, so they came up to him and said, "You seem not to have had as much to drink as the other guys," and this insulted Ab. He said, "Hell, man, I've had as much to drink as all these guys put together."

Eventually, they finally let them go, even after a comment like that, and they got on the interstate and they decided they could drive better with their lights off than on, since it was a clear night with a full moon, and they ran off the road into a ditch, and we had to go dig 'em out, you know.

~~~

In 1968 when many college students were burning flags and protesting the Vietnam War, I was at Cumberland College. There was a great story that came out of this phenomena of burning the flag. I was able to garner a flag from Dr. Tim Lee Carter, our fifth district of Kentucky representative, that had flown over the U.S. Capitol. And then I was able to take it to Frankfort, Kentucky, where Gov. Louie Nunn had the flag flown over the State Capitol. At some point that flag was presented to me, and I enlisted the cross country team to run this flag 150 miles back to the Cumberland College basketball game that was goin' on and pass it on to the president, Dr. J.M. Boswell.

This made national news, and as a result of that run we were invited to come and meet Col. Patton, who was the son of Gen. George Patton, who was at the University of Louisville ROTC. A night or two after we delivered this flag to Cumberland, the ROTC Building at the University of Louisville was burned to the ground. When Col. Patton heard about our run, he immediately called Cumberland and asked for a few of us to come up to Louisville, and we did that, and during that time he gave me a picture of his father urinating in the Rhine. Evidently Gen. Patton had said all across France and when they invaded Germany that by a certain date, "I'll be peein' in the Rhine." And I have that picture in my office for anybody that wants to see it.

But we made the news for several days by just doing what we thought was patriotic and, instead of burning the flag, we cherished it and carried it to the college and flew it over

Members of the Cumberland College cross-country team returned a flag to Cumberland after it flew at the state capitol in Frankfort.

the campus for several weeks. It was a great event and a great accomplishment.

~~~

Abner made some very big impressions on the people at Cumberland College. There was a young lady who was president of the Baptist Student Union. She was an attractive Italian girl who came to Cumberland College because, I guess, she was Baptist.

Anyway, Abner enticed her to go out on a date with him and, of course, Abner was driving the old cattle truck. So he loaded her up in the old cattle truck after dinner one night, and he took her out to a place called Bonn Holler.

Now Bonn Holler was a famous parking place. Now the girl did not understand exactly what was goin' on out there. But as she looked around in the other cars she saw a lot of stuff she didn't exactly agree with, so she asked Abner to take her back to the dormitory.

So he goes back over to the dormitory and parks and goes into the setting room with her. Now Cumberland at that time had big Victorian rooms on the first floor where men and women could watch TV and sit around and talk. So she went upstairs to freshen herself up, and when she came back downstairs, she suspected Ab had been drinkin' and chewing tobacco. So she threw him out of the dormitory.

I was a resident assistant at Mahan Hall, and Ab come mopin' in that night, and I asked him what was wrong, and he told me what had happened to him that evening. He went through all that I aforementioned, and he got to the point where she was comin' down the stairs and she said, "Abner Lipps, you must leave immediately!" And she followed him over to the door, and, as he was leaving, here's what he told me: "She looked at me, and she said, 'Abner Lipps, you have no couth!'"

And Abner looked at me, and he said, "Crap, Ray, ain't I got couth?" I said, "Abner, you got couth. Don't worry about it. She don't know what she's talkin' about."

~~~

74

One of my roommates at Cumberland was my friend Ralph Lynch. We were resident assistants of Mahan Hall, and we ended up living together in Suite 125, which was a two-room suite on the first floor, for a couple years together, and Ralph and I became fast friends. In my auction business, I've run an auction for Cumberland for thirty-five years, and Ralph's not missed a time helping me to put that auction on. He's been very loyal to Cumberland, and he's been very loyal to me. And he was a pretty good straight man.

My friend Lloyd Abdoo had this big, long limousine, and we came rolling into town into Williamsburg in that limousine, and my friend Ralph was the state probation and parole officer in the county. So we came rolling into town, went to his office and picked him up and took him out to eat, and on the way back to his office it occurred to us that he was uncomfortable with that limousine parked in front of his office.

So he asked us, he said, "Do you guys mind dropping me off on the other side of the bridge?" So as we were dropping him off, I said, "Ralph, one thing. If Lloyd and I should get into trouble – which we don't think we're going to – but if we should have some trouble in life and we get arrested for something, will you be our probation and parole officer?

And Ralph studied that carefully, and he said, "I think you boys are gonna go federal."

Me and my best friend Lloyd Abdoo

There is a story about when the three of us graduated from Cumberland in 1970. The local newspaper wrote a nice story about me, Ray, graduating; and then they wrote a nice story about Ralph; and then in small print after those two stories were printed, in a column they said this single sentence: Their brother Abner also graduated.

~~~

Graduation day. From left are Ralph, Joe, Susie, Ray and Abner.

One of my cohorts and I had a goal when we got out of college: We wanted to make $30,000 each by the time we were 30 years old. That seemed like an admirable goal at the time.

Well, we had good news and bad news. The good news was most of us made $30,000 a year by the time we were 30 years old. The bad news is it didn't buy much. So you young folks, set your goals a little higher than we did.

~~~

After graduation, I accepted a job at Cumberland as admissions and public relations officer. And after I'd been there about two and a half years, I decided Gov. Louie Nunn was gonna run for Senate, and I had been working on his behalf for a number of years while I was in the

College Republicans and the Young Republicans, and I had an opportunity to get involved along with Mike Duncan and some of the other college Republican Federation people. So I made the rash decision to join the campaign and go work the last few days of Gov. Nunn's governorship and get involved in his run for Senate, which proved to be unsuccessful. So I decided to leave Cumberland College, where I'd been for seven years, and go out into the world and join the Louie Nunn for Senate campaign.

As I was moving stuff out of my office – my office was straight across the hall from Dr. B's office – he saw me loadin' my stuff up, and he came down into the parking lot and he told me he hated to see me leave.

He said, "You're good for Cumberland, and you could do great things here. Jim Taylor's gonna be president someday, I'm sure, and you would get along with him and move along pretty quickly. So my advice to you is to stay right where you are. But if you have made a decision, I will support it. But I will tell you that as long as I'm alive, if you want a job it'll be available to you."

And then he pulled out two hundred dollars and gave them to me, and he said, "I don't require that you give these back to me. In fact, I'd be hurt if you did. But I know where you're going, and charity begins at home, so I want you to take these two hundred dollars and use it to get set up."

Dr. Boswell was ten feet tall when I came, and he was ten

feet tall when I left. Over the years, we wrote back and forth many times, and every so often I drag out all those letters and I read 'em all. And I still enjoy them.

Cumberland cohorts included Mike Duncan, Roger Baker, Ron Glass, John Heneison and Earl Brady.

~~~

There was a time at Cumberland College when we changed the name of our teams and mascots from the Indians to the Patriots. Some people my age raised cain about that; they didn't understand why we did that. They falsely assumed we did that because of political correctness. They could not have been further from the truth.

Dr. Taylor intended Williamsburg, Kentucky, to be the other Williamsburg, and he built buildings on campus to match the buildings over in Williamsburg, Virginia. We made every effort to be on Interstate 75 and to call ourselves the other Williamsburg. So there was a good reason to change it from the Indians to the Patriots. Over the years it's proven to be a very good decision.

Nevertheless, there were people who thought it was the wrong thing to do. And there were many big arguments and meetings at Cumberland, and people expressed their opinions one way or the other.

There was a time I was given an award at Cumberland when a room was named after me in the business department, and it was very appropriate for me to coin this phrase since it was at a building that was a copy of Constitution Hall in Williamsburg, Virginia. So when I began my speech, I said, "I am proud to be a graduate of the University of the Cumberlands, where all the Indians are Patriots." That phrase will forever stick as the explanation of our mascot. I'm proud to have coined that phrase.

~~~

I served on Cumberland's Alumni Board of Directors for more than 20 years, and over those years I was honored many times and in many ways. It was very rewarding. I started the homecoming auction which has raised many dollars for the university, and I was one of the founders of the Athletic Hall of Fame, and I funded all the plaques by having a small auction before.

As far as awards to me, in 1989 when daughter Denise and David Bergman were graduating from Cumberland, I was inducted into the Alumni Hall of Honor. I thought that was probably the greatest honor I would ever get. There was a lady there who had cancer and who spoke before me, and she got up and covered pretty much all the students she had ever had – which was her prerogative – and she took a long time to thank the college for the award she was getting. However, she took so much time to thank the college that I felt like people were getting antsy, so I forgot about the speech I was going to give. I said, "A famous author said that everybody would have 15 minutes in the limelight and if that be true, then this be mine."

I had a couple of basketball players who came up to me after the ceremony was over and said, "Well, we came to hear a good speech by an old friend, and you ended up giving a lousy speech by an artist that we don't agree with, and it was the worst speech we ever heard in our life." I said, "Well, boys, I'm sorry you feel that way, but I didn't feel like I had much time to say anything; I did the best I could." A little later on in the evening I saw Dr. Taylor, and he came along and put his arm around me and said, "That was one of the best speeches I ever heard. You were putting all your eggs in one basket, and it was a great speech." So there were the two versions, and I've chosen to accept Dr. Taylor's version over the other version.

So that was the beginning of a long record of having auctions and contributing any way I could to Cumberland

College. I have brought over 200 students to the college, and that's probably the greatest thing anybody could do for Cumberland is to bring them a good student. I will admit I brought some that weren't the best students Cumberland ever had, but on the other hand, I'm starting to get a lot of students who are very good.

The next thing I can remember that happened, there was a time when the college built a new business building, the Hutton School of Business. And one day they called me up from the college, and they said Dr. Taylor and the board of directors have agreed to name a room in your honor in that building. I was overwhelmed. But that's what happened. I went up, and there was 150 people there in the hallway. There on the second floor is a room dedicated to Ray Lipps. And I thought, this must be the highest honor I will ever get. Another 15 minutes in the limelight, you know.

And then there was the time Dr Taylor came to my house, and we were sittin' there havin' lunch, and Dr. Taylor said, "I'm going to give you an honorary doctorate, a doctorate of fine arts." Over the next few weeks and months they started gathering information about me, things I'd done while I was in college, and things I'd done after I left college, and it added up to a litany of accomplishments, so I gave them a list of people who might want to attend, and they told me that over 200 people showed up that day, and of course around 4,000 students were there.

I honored my sister-in-law that day by starting a scholarship fund for Judy Lipps, and there was some contributions to that that day, and I named each of the children in the crowd by sharing the year they would graduate from Cumberland if they were students in the future. Phil Lowe's little boy was the class of '33, and that made a lot of newspaper coverage, and many papers wrote about the class of '33. I donated to the college a set of engravings of the first 24 U.S. presidents, and they're hanging someplace on campus, I'm sure.

So I figured how in the world can I be honored more than that day. But they figured a way to do it. Dave Bergman came up with a way to do it. In October 2013 they renamed the University of the Cumberlands Hall of Honor the Ray Lipps Hall of Honor. And the first inductee into that Hall was my best friend Lloyd Abdoo. It was another day that was surely my last 15 minutes in the limelight.

I was invited to give the homecoming keynote speech at Cumberland in 1992.

FAMILY

My grandfather, Abner Mahler, came to the United States on a whim. He was from a well-to-do family and he hid out on a boat and came in as a stowaway.

He started a business where he had a wagon, and he had a horse named Mike, and he got up early in the morning and went to the bakery. He had to deal with the bakery every day, and he had a route where he delivered this bread and maybe made a few pennies on each loaf. He was an entrepreneur and lived by his wits, as I have, and my father did.

I have seen a shoe that Mike wore. My Uncle Marty in New York has one of Mike's shoes over his door. I have seen it and touched it from Mike the horse.

~~~

My grandfather Jim Grab Lipps lived by his wits, as my father lived by his wits, and I have lived by my wits. Lloyd's grandfather lived by his wits, his father lived by his wits and Lloyd lived by his wits. So Lloyd Abdoo and Ray Lipps have carried on the tradition of working for ourselves and making our way as we could, and we were somewhat successful at makin' a good livin'.

My grandfather Jim Lipps would buy up stuff all month in the community he lived in – he would buy up loose cattle and horses and sometimes geese; whatever he thought he could make a buck on, you know – he would load 'em all up and drive 'em to Richmond, Kentucky, which was forty-two miles from where he lived, and he would sell 'em at auction or sell 'em to some individual, and the next month he would come back and do that very same thing again.

My father bought and sold cattle his whole life; he would go out and look for cattle in the community, and he would buy anything he thought he could make some money on, and he would bring 'em into the auction sales at the end of the week, and he would sell 'em. He had a partner named Roy Brewer, and they were a well-made match; they both knew a lot about the cattle, and they both were eager to buy and make money as best they could.

Myself, I've been through thick and thin, but I've lived in such a way that I've been able to make contributions to my college, to my church, to the Lions Club, and I've made the money to help all these projects because I've lived by my wits. Lloyd has the same kind of testimonial. Sometimes we didn't have the money to buy gas to get to a closing but in general we've lived better than most, and gave away a lot of money and took care of a lot of people, and we lived by our wits and were successful at it.

Jim Lipps, a trader and my grandfather

~~~

One of the great things I remember about my grandfather is when I was a child he would set in front of the fireplace whenever we would visit, and he would chew tobacco and spit into the fireplace from time to time, which would create a sizzle and a pleasant smell, really, and he would tell us stories about the time he bought 200 geese and took the wagon in case some of 'em got tired, and by the time he got to Richmond they were all tired and all on the wagon, and told us stories about people trying to rob him. We couldn't wait to get back to hear my grandfather's stories.

I don't think I was ever there when he didn't have a fire in that fireplace in the living room, and the walls were covered up with Sears and Roebuck leaves. It was truly a place to hear fantastic stories which we believed then and I have no reason to believe to this day are not true.

~~~

My Aunt Martha came down from New York each summer to spend a couple of months with her sister, and when my mother passed away the Spit and Whittle Club kind of moved into the house from up at the courthouse, but my aunt continued to come down and visit Joe for a couple of months during the summertime. And it was during these times I would take Joe and Martha over to my Uncle Sam's house to visit with him.

Now my Uncle Sam had a stroke when he was in his early 50s and he lived to be in his late 80s. He was by himself a lot, and Joe liked to go visit him, and I enjoyed taking him over there.

It was on such an afternoon that Sam's wife Edna's brother — Leander Wagers, was his name – came over that afternoon to visit with him also. My Aunt Martha was taken with the name Leander; she thought it was a fantastic name; it was even odd for Clay County. Clay County had a lot of odd stuff goin' on over there, but this name was unique.

So they were having a discussion on one of these trips, and my Aunt Martha asked Leander, she said, "Leander, what do you attribute your longevity to?" Of course, I had to interpret to Leander what the question was, so I said, "Well, she's asking you a question: How have you lived so long?"

Leander looked like an Irish sage. He had one of those Irish hats on, and he smoked a small pipe and he puffed on it, and he reflected on any question he was asked; he was slow to answer, and he studied on how he would answer the question and put some time into it.

And so he puffed a time or two on his pipe, and he looked up at the sky, and he said to my Aunt Martha, he said, "Salt. I eat a lot of salt. It purifies the body."

I could see the wheels turning in my aunt's mind, you know, and she could think of nothing else but the kind of discussion she was going to have on the way home with me about how he had answered that question. So, first thing when we got in the car, she started to say something, and I said, "Martha, don't go there." So we never discussed it again. But if you want to know how to live a long life, eat a lot of salt. It purifies the body.

~~~

Sammy Lipps is my second cousin. My grandfather is his great-grandfather. My uncle Sam is his grandfather. And Sammy is younger than I am by a few years.

One day several years ago as a young fellow he was out riding around and he decided to visit the cabin where my grandfather lived his life on Double Creek in Clay County, Kentucky. And he went up there and was lookin' at the house – lookin' at the logs and lookin' at the well; it actually had Sears and Roebuck pages on the walls of the house, and most of the furniture was still there. And he noticed that the back door stood slightly open, so he pushed it – nobody had lived there for several years – so he went on in the house just to look around and to see what he could remember from when he used to go there.

Scanning the main room he saw this box and looked in it, and it was a bunch of letters from my father Joe Lipps and my uncle John Lipps from during WWII, and lots of pictures. So he took it home and showed it to his mother. And she said, "You take that back! That doesn't belong to you; that belongs to the Lippses." (She was talking about the older Lippses.) She scolded him and said, "You take that back at your earliest convenience."

So within a couple of weeks he decided that he would go back over there and put that box back in the main room of that house, but when he got there, unfortunately – but it turned out to be fortunately – the house had burned to the ground.

So as a result of him doing something his mother thought was wrong, he salvaged some two hundred twenty-five pictures and documents, and it really added to the history of our family. Sammy did a great deed that day, and he's started to collect things related to our family, and he's a very successful young man. Thank you, Sammy.

~~~

We had many family reunions as we became older. We had a reunion – and continue to do so — on the third Saturday of June, which is my brothers' and my birthdays, and my mother's birthday was in June, and a sister-in-law's and a couple of the grandchildrens' birthdays were in June, so we just naturally migrated to that time.

So we went up to the park or we ate out, and for years I fixed the dinner for that group. And there was 50 or 60 people who would come, and there was a weird conglomeration of people involved there. There was people who would not drive the main highway to the reunion. There was people who would not eat turkey. There was people who would not eat biscuits; they'd eat cornbread instead. And there was all kinds of oddities in our family, so to speak.

One of the things that would happen is my mother was there in her wheelchair, and she'd keep her pocketbook slung over the back of that wheelchair, and three or four times during that family reunion she would call me over and say, "Is my pocketbook okay?" And I always wondered about that. I would say, "But you gotta watch these Lippses; somebody will pilfer your pocketbook before you get home, so check it often."

I wondered why she asked us that question all the time. I think – I don't know this for sure – but when she passed away there was maybe a lot of hundred dollar bills in that pocketbook, some might guess maybe sixty of 'em.

~~~

My Uncle Marty is a fantastic human being. He's been blind for some 70 years or so, and he's an engineer, and he had a small factory – he may have had 30 people working for him at one time or another – and he invented things, and he made things out of tubular aluminum. And one of the things he made is the Mahler Cane, which is the cane used by most blind people. It's a cane that has one-foot, or maybe 18-inch, sections of aluminum, tapered toward the bottom. It's got an elastic bungee cord-type thing in the center, and when you are done using it, it folds up and you can stick it in a little bag on your belt, and when you need the cane, you take it out and kind of whip it and it all bounces back together and makes a feeler cane. And my uncle invented that and sold a bunch of 'em and lives in a brownstone in Flatbush in Brooklyn.

There are hundreds of stories I could tell about my uncle; he always is upbeat and whenever I talk to him he says, "You're lookin' good," and he's done everything from ski to inventing a rail that fits on the side of a bowling lane, and you slide your hand down it, and it allows blind people to bowl. He was pretty good at it himself, I think. At some time he came down to Cincinnati for a bowling championship. There were five people on the team and either two or three had to be totally blind, and the other two or three had to be legally blind.

I remember him comin' down to visit our farm, and before he left, we had a field — it was kind of a ridge — and there was a valley there with water, and before he left he went down in the valley and had us all stand up on that ridge on a sunny afternoon, and he could see the outline of us, I guess. I think that was maybe the last thing he saw, and that was a long time ago.

But he's still alive, and he's still aggressively writing poetry and he has his classes, and he loves every day of life, and he's an inspiration to all the people who know him.

~~~

My uncle Marty is a poet, and over the last few years he has published several books of poetry. He teaches poetry whenever the opportunity arises, and he recently wrote a fantastic book that covers some of the history of our family.

My uncle Marty is my mother's brother; there were two girls and a boy in that family. My mother was oldest, her sister Martha was next, and my uncle Marty was the youngest. Each of them had many talents. All of the three of them had three children, so there are nine cousins. We have all led quite different lives, but we're all intelligent.

When I got this latest book from my uncle, I opened it up by chance and there was a poem called "Lost on Becker Street." I read the poem, and it was a takeoff on Robert Frost's "The Road Not Taken."

> *"Two roads diverged in a yellow wood,*
> *And sorry I could not travel both*
> *And be one traveler, long I stood*
> *And looked down one as far as I could*
> *To where it bent in the undergrowth;*
>
> *Then took the other, as just as fair,*
> *And having perhaps the better claim,*
> *Because it was grassy and wanted wear;*
> *Though as for that the passing there*
> *Had worn them really about the same...*

His poem talked about how Fourth Street crossed over Tenth Street in Brooklyn, where he lived. His poem had visions of Frost, and he couldn't understand how Fourth Street could cross over Tenth Street, and he didn't know why that was and he didn't know which one to take – to continue on Tenth Street or to continue on Fourth Street, so he wrote a poem about it, and in the poem he eventually says that he took the wrong street and that's why he's now lost on Becker Street.

So when he gets my Christmas letter, he usually calls me up and we discuss some of the things that are in my Christmas letter, so I was waiting for the call in the days before Christmas, and one day the phone rang and I knew it was him, and I picked up the phone, and he said, "How're you doing, Ray?" and I said, "I'm lost on Becker Street." And he said, "You read my book!" I did not admit that I had not read all his book, because it made his day that I answered the phone that way.

~~~

My uncle enjoyed humor. There was a time we went to visit him in New York – my two brothers and I – he lived in Flatbush in one of the brownstones there. He had invented the cane that blind people use, and he'd made a lot of money in the process and had invested it well, and he lived in an exclusive area of Brooklyn, and we were all there, and he decided that we would walk up to this Greek restaurant and eat dinner that night. It was about a mile and a half away, so we were all out on the sidewalk walkin' together – his three girls, and us three guys and a couple of our other cousins, we were all there walkin' up the street toward this Greek restaurant.

And on the way my Uncle Marty was teaching us a Greek greeting; you know, what we'd say when we got there. He said the owner of the restaurant would be out greeting people as they came into the restaurant, so he had us practice all the way to the restaurant this Greek greeting.

Unbeknownst to him, the Greek guy had sold the restaurant to a Chinese guy so the Chinese guy was out there greeting people. My uncle did not know there'd been a change, and being blind he could not see the change, so we all gave this Greek greeting, and the Chinese guy looked at us all like he thought we were crazy, you know. When we told my uncle what we'd done, he thought it was the funniest thing in the world.

~~~

Denise came up with the perfect name for stories by Ab: Aboriginals. So any story told by Ab since we were little boys can be referred to as an Aboriginal.

~~~

At Denise and Mart's wedding, with my late wife Bella.

I was by myself after Bella died for about three years. I was down at the church, and they were building that addition on the back of the church. Bella had wanted to be a part of it, and she wanted us to donate ten percent of it, which was about forty thousand dollars, or close to it. So I decided to have this auction. I got all my auctioneer friends in, and we had this big auction. And I think we raised twenty-three thousand dollars that day.

But that morning before the auction that evening, I was down there at the church, and Pat's uncle had died – Pat's brother and I were friends for 35 years, close friends. Well, Pat and I had crossed paths, but nobody had ever introduced me to her. So they came by the church before

97

the auction — I had a suit on, driving a Cadillac, you know, as flamboyant as I usually am, you know. So Jack brought his sister Pat and his other sister into the church to look at our collection because she was looking for a piece of art.

So she looked around, and that afternoon Jack called and said, "My sister wants to look at more art up at your gallery." I said, "Well, Jack, I'm pretty busy, you know, but I'll do that."

So we met up at the office up there, and I had these Books on Tape – I was making trips up to Philadelphia every few weeks, and I'd listen to two tapes up and two tapes back. I had every one of the John Grisham books, you know, and Pat said she read those. And she picked out a piece of art, and I said, "Are there some there you haven't read?" And she said yeah, and I said, "Go ahead and take 'em and you can ship 'em back to me." So she did that.

There's a side story or two here – on the way home, Jack told Pat, "You know, Ray's interested in you." She said, "No, he's not. You guys are crazy." Jack said, "Well, I've known Ray a long time, and he seemed interested in you." Jack's wife, Carolyn, who never has anything to say about such matters, chimed in and said, "I noticed it, too!"

So Pat goes home and throws up. It makes her so nervous that she actually throws up.

So Jack calls me on Thursday and said, "You call my sister yet?" And I said, "No, I haven't done that." He said, "Well, give her a call." So I said, "What's her number?" and he gave me the number and I called her up.

Now there's a hundred stories that could be told here, like the time she calls me up one Saturday early on and says, "Don't call me till after 9:30 tonight because I'm going to be out antiquing with a friend of mine; we're going to an auction and this, that and the other."

So I thought, "Nine thirty. It's two o'clock now. It's a six-and-a-half or seven hour drive over there. I can be there before nine-thirty."

So I was backin' out of my driveway and I see this black car across the road from me, and it's blinkin' its lights. And I get out on Clinton Highway and they pull up behind me and start blinkin' their lights again. Well, I pulled off the side of the road, and they pulled up behind me and Jack got out – it was his wife's car, and I didn't recognize it. Jack got out and came up to the window – it was raining pretty good – and said, "What're you doin' today?" And I said, "I'm goin' over to see your sister." And Carolyn said, "Great! I'll call her and tell her you're coming so she can fix her hair." And I said, "No, don't tell her I'm comin'. This is a surprise." The last thing I saw in my rearview mirror was Carolyn holding her right hand up and Jack making her swear she wouldn't call. In the rain.

So I drive as hard as I can and I get over to Charlottesville to her driveway, and I see her garage is open and her car's in the garage. And I pulled up – she lived in one of these modern duplexes – and it was kind of a long house, and the garage was at the end. So she couldn't see the driveway, in other words.

So I called her up on my cellphone and I said, "I'm in your driveway. Come out and get me," and she said, "No, you're not in my driveway." (This has to do with Pat's rules.) I said, "Well, I am in your driveway," and she said, "Well, come on in then." I said, "No, I'm not comin' in til you believe I'm in your driveway. I'm in your driveway, and I'm tellin' you I'm in your driveway. Just come on out."

She said, "No, I'm not gonna do that. You're not in my driveway. There's no way anybody would drive up here to see me and not tell me you're coming. It ain't happening and I'm not gonna be conned into believing it."

I said, "Pat, get up and walk in your bedroom and look out the damn window!" She said, "No, I'm not gonna do that. You're not there." I said, "Well, if you get up and walk to the bedroom and I'm not there, who is gonna know besides you?" She said, "I'll know, and I'm not gonna do that."

There was a woman who lived next door to her who had this little dog. She'd throw that little dog out in the yard when she saw my car pull up, and then she'd come outside looking for the dog and look at me. I told Pat if she didn't come out I was gonna see what her neighbor was doing that evening.

So somehow, she had this little thing in the kitchen like a bay window and if you leaned up in that and looked back, you could see my car. So finally, finally, she saw my car, and she said, "Get in here!" I told her the moral of this story is if I'm in your parking lot again and call you and tell you I'm there and you don't come outside, rest assured I'll be down at your mailbox nekkid and playin' a guitar, so don't leave me out there very long.

Her whole family waited at her mother's house to see how this visit would come out, I'm tellin' you. I brought her family to life. They never met, they never went out together, they never went to each other's house. Pat had never been in Jack's house. So I brought 'em all together, and Pat's mother thanked me every day for bringing Pat home.

Pat just read one of Ray's stories.

Pat and I were married at 12:01 a.m. on January 1, 2000. At our left is Judy and Ralph, and on the right are Connie and Abner.

Denise and Cole

The Sesler family: Denise, center; Jordan,
left; Mart, right, and Cole.

CHARACTERS AND ADVENTURES

For years and years and years I had a fellow working for me named Roy Strange. Now Roy was an excellent worker; he was in jail from time to time, so I had to go and get him out of jail here and there, but he always did me right – most of the time. Most of the time Roy did what he should in life, and he was a hard worker. He didn't have any education; he couldn't read and write but he pushed forward in the world. He always had a job, and he had some deal workin', and I had a relationship with him for maybe 25 years.

The way I met him, I had these two young fellas workin' for me during the World's Fair, and I saw this guy come walking through the campground – we were working at a campground – and I saw this fella come walkin' through and come walkin' up toward us, and I said, "Who's this axe murderer?" And one of 'em said, "He's our brother." So that's how I met him. I nicknamed him Axe Murderer, and we shortened that down to Axe, and when you put that together, that's Axe Strange.

We called him Axe for so many years, to the point that his mother knew him as Axe and everybody knew him as Axe Strange. There was a time when he had this little person who ran around with him – a dwarf, I guess – and they worked together and bid on jobs together, and naturally we named him Hatchet. So it was Axe and Hatchet.

When I was dating my present wife Pat, I threatened her with Axe and Hatchet dressin' up in tuxedos and throwing down a pillow right outside her office, and me gettin' down on one knee and proposing right there. And she thought we might do that.

~~~

I am an avid barterer. There was a time I bartered for a whole pallet of physician's scales – the stand-up scales that cost five or six hundred dollars each. I had a whole pallet of 'em.

The fellow working for me, his name was Roy Strange. And Roy came to me one day and said, "I'd like to talk you outta one of those physician's scales." I said, "What would you do with one of those physician's scales? They're five or six hundred dollars apiece." He said, "Well, I'm wantin' to weigh my pig."

I said, "Well, how are you fixin' to weigh your pig on a physician's scale? You just gonna say, 'Pig, get on that scale?' I don't think that's gonna work." He said, "Well, uh, how would you do it?"

I said, "Well, first thing I'd do is weigh Roy Strange, and I'd make a note of what that amount might be. Then I'd have Roy Strange catch the pig and get on the scales with the pig in arm, and I would record the Roy-and-pig weight. And when that was done I would subtract Roy from Roy-and-pig, and the resulting weight would be the pig. That's how I would do it."

Roy looked at me and said, "That's too much trouble. Just forget I asked."

~~~

When Lloyd Abdoo, my best friend, came to town, it was our tradition that we would sleep in the kingsize bed that we had, and Bella would move into the guest bedroom for the two or three days that he was there, and Lloyd and I would watch old movies and kind of rest up for the next trip, and we would eat pizzas and popcorn and generally have a relaxing evening or two before Lloyd went back on the road.

At some point, Pat heard about this; someone told her that Bella moved out of the bedroom when Lloyd was there, so she came to me, and she said, "I'll tell you what, when that Abdoo guy shows up I ain't movin' out of the bedroom," and I said, "Well, Lloyd won't mind," and she said, "What does that mean?" And I said, "Well, it means that he won't mind."

~~~

The Sponge: That's a nickname that I gave to Craig Hendricks who served as interim pastor at our church while we were searching for a pastor a few years ago. I called him The Sponge and he called me The Heathen. I think we were both quite correct.

I call him The Sponge because he has the kind of mind that soaks up everything around him. Even if he is sitting at a table eating at a restaurant, he is listening to the conversation beside of him, in front of him; he's like a sponge, he takes in everything around him.

There was a time I called him one Saturday morning; I had a crew in Chattanooga working an art sale. On Friday when we set it up, I didn't feel well, so I didn't go. But on Saturday I started feeling better but I didn't feel well enough to drive. So I called up Craig Hendricks, and I said, "Craig, do you know of anybody who would want to drive one of my cars and go down to Chattanooga for a show we're having down there?" and he said, "I will; I'll do that. I'll be happy to do that."

So it was a great ride down there. We stopped and ate lunch, and when we finally got to Chattanooga the sale was going full blast, and I was sellin' stuff and Philip Lowe was sellin' stuff, and I looked over and Craig was sellin' stuff. He got right into it, just like he owned the factory. We had a very successful day, and we ate a big supper, and we got back to the church and the Boy Scouts were having a dinner of some sort, and Pastor Craig went in and had dinner with the Boy Scouts. And later on that evening, he had a Guess Who's Coming to Dinner over at Kay's house, so I know he ate about five times that day. He doesn't have a lot of weight on him, so I don't know, maybe he has a lot of nervous energy.

The Sponge is one of the captains of the Powell Yacht Club, and he certainly has a lot of suggestions for that. He calls me The Heathen; I'm not sure why, but he's not far off. I can be classified as a heathen from time to time. We enjoy each other's company and we enjoy each other's tales, and there's a possibility, just a slim possibility, that we may tell big lies from time to time.

~~~

There was a man in my church at Powell Presbyterian named Bob White. Bob and I were in church together for about twenty years.

About sixteen years into that time, a guy came into my office one day and pulled up a chair and set down at my desk and said, "I want to ask you some questions." And for the life of me, I couldn't think who he was. I knew that I'd seen his face somewhere, but I couldn't place it. I tried to do the old hang-in-here-and-have-a-discussion-until-you-can-figure-out-what's-going-on, so I was in the process of trying to figure out who this man was that was sitting at my desk. At some point I realized I go to church with this man. I finally remembered his name, and that day we began a conversation that lasted for four years.

Bob told me that he had come to my office to discuss his father. He said he'd heard that I was involved with the University of the Cumberlands in Williamsburg, Kentucky, previously known as Cumberland College. He told me that his father was captain of the football team and captain of the basketball team in 1921, and he wondered if this was the kind of information I would like to have. I'm a sitting member of the Athletic Hall of Fame committee, so I was very interested in finding out about Bob's dad.

 The next day he brought me a diploma and he brought me several newspaper articles about his father; his father had scored 17 points against University of Kentucky and beat 'em by himself. That year he beat UK, he beat UT, he beat Louisville, he beat Eastern Kentucky University, which was called Eastern Kentucky Normal School; it was there in print. It helped us make a decision; we thought we were the Redhounds during those years, turns out we were the Mountaineers, and I made every effort to get Bob's father inducted into the Athletic Hall of Fame at Cumberland College. I was unable to do that. There were some people on the board that were purists, and they didn't want to accept the documentation of the newspaper, and they disagreed with me that this was the sort of accomplishment that would put him in the Hall of Fame. I thought it was, and I'm not done with that yet. I'm still going to pursue that for a few more years.

But Bob was happy with what we did do. The day the college gave me a doctorate they also inducted Bob's father into the University of the Cumberlands Hall of Honor. Bob, his daughter and his brother were there to receive the award for his father, and Bob gave an eloquent acceptance speech.

And so we began a four-year conversation about places we'd been together; we came up with a couple of times when we'd been in the same room, or in the same building or on the same grounds. There was a helicopter wreck where a lawyer had gotten his arm cut off, and he was there and I was there.

Bob had cancer and he fought it for four long years. His wife had died of cancer four years before his demise. We talked about everything under the sun, and I told Pat I'm going to do my best to get him out of the house. And I invited him over to watch a ballgame and eat hamburgers, and whenever we had an event at our house – a chicken dinner or a low country boil or my birthday – we'd call Bob and ask him if he'd like to join us, and he'd say, "I'll be there." He honored us by being at our events. And we all will miss Bob.

~~~

A couple of friends of mine were on their way back from a meeting in Nashville, and my friend David was driving along enjoying the drive and his wife was in the back seat. And there was a time when David looked in the rearview mirror and there was a blue light behind him.

He immediately pulled off the road, and the state trooper got out and came up to the driver's side and he said, "Sir, sir, did you know there was a woman who fell out of your car about four miles back?"

And David hit himself on the side of the head and said, "Thank goodness! For a while there I thought I went deaf!"

~~~

This past year on Christmas Eve for some reason my wife went to check the front door. And when she opened the door she was surprised to see a huge box sittin' in front of the door.

So she dragged it inside, and it was filled up with all kinds of goodies; it had oranges and apples and candies of all sorts – some of it sugar-free, so it was somebody who knew us pretty well. It was crammed full of things to eat on the day before Christmas.

Now what's rare about this and what makes it an interesting story is it didn't say who it was from. Nobody took credit for it. There was no card on it that said Enjoy or whatever; it was just a boxful of stuff sittin' on our front porch.

We thought it was a fantastic idea, and we plan on doing it ourselves in the future, and we wish we would've thought of it, although a long time ago my coach and I used to set oranges on people's front porches. So I was very intrigued by this, and so we started to think about who might do this, and we came up with about 65 friends who might do something like that. And we were impressed that we knew 65 people who were nice enough to have done something like that.

So we asked a lot of people, and nobody 'fessed up to it, and it's been six or seven months since that happened, and to this day nobody's admitted to putting that on our porch. I still find that intriguing and fascinating and wish that I'd thought of it myself. So next year if you find something on your front porch, it might be from me.

~ ~ ~

This story is about my bout with gambling. When I was a young feller working in the governor's office of Kentucky, there was a lot of older people there trying to teach us younger people what we could do and we couldn't do. So one night they invited me and a couple other people my age to a poker game.

I had never played poker in my life, and I lost ninety dollars that night. It took part of my rent money, and it was months getting even to where I could do anything because of paying that ninety dollars off. I vowed I would never gamble again.

So anyway, there was a time I was going to Las Vegas for a business meeting, and I told a friend of mine who is a gambler that I was going to Las Vegas but I didn't intend to gamble. And he said, "Well, what you should do – how much did you lose?" I said, "I lost ninety bucks a long time ago, and I vowed I wouldn't gamble again." He said, "What you should do is collect all the loose money you got and go out to Las Vegas and put it on a color on the roulette wheel." I said, "I don't know much about that," and he said, "Well, watch it for a while and figure out how you can make a bet, and make one more bet and either make your money back or figure out you're not a gambler for sure."

It sounded like a plausible plan to me, so I went out to Vegas and I had about two hundred and twenty-five dollars that I'd saved up, and I decided to watch the roulette wheel, and I watched it for a long time. And I came up with a theory about how I could get my money back. I could watch the wheel until it landed on a color five times in a row – either it was red five times in a row, or it was black five times in a row — and if that happened, on the sixth time I would put it on the opposite color.

So I watched and watched and watched, and I had on a suit and tie, and everybody else was pretty casually dressed. And they didn't know who I was, and I didn't have any chips. I just put down two hundred and twenty-five dollars eventually, so I watched and eventually it was red five times in a row, and I put my money down, and I said, "Black." And everybody there changed their bets to black; they thought I knew something more than they did.

It's such a fickle thing; everybody's looking for an edge and betting that I know what I'm doing, and I'd never made a bet in my life in a casino. But they were willing to follow what I'm doing, maybe because they thought it would bring them luck also. And in that case it did. It came up black, and I won the bet – two hundred and twenty five dollars — and I did not stick to that thing I said I would do and never bet again. I went back over to the basketball game that was going on. It was halftime and Kentucky was playing, and I bet a hundred dollars that Kentucky would win, and I won that bet, too.

So there's the two bets that I won in my life gambling in Las Vegas. I've been back there three or four times since then, and I've never placed another bet.

~~~

There was a time when I lived in Corbin, Kentucky, in a subdivision called Tatersal in a really nice home. And I was sitting in front of the fireplace one night – it was a cold winter evening – and at that time I lived by myself, and I heard my best friend Lloyd Abdoo knock at the door. He was at my door; it was just about the edge of dark, and I invited him in, and we fixed a sandwich and were sitting in front of the fireplace, and Lloyd said, "Would it be all right if I spent the night here?" and I said, "Absolutely, Lloyd. Absolutely. I'm honored that you're here and that you'd stay the night with me."

So he said, "I think I'll just bed down here in front of the fireplace, and I'll see you at breakfast."

So we got up the next morning, and Lloyd told me, we were eatin' breakfast, and Lloyd said, "I need a favor, Ray." And I said, "What can I do for you, Lloyd?" He said, "I'm goin' up to Pikeville, Kentucky, to buy this motel; they're wantin' three million dollars for it." I believe he told me three million dollars, and he said, "I'm gonna go buy that, and I need your help."

And I was thinkin' how can I help somebody who needs three million dollars to buy a motel? What is he thinkin', you know, that I could help in that situation? What in the world could I do to further that deal? And I couldn't think of any way that I could help that deal.

And I said, "Lloyd, for the life of me I can't fathom what I could do to help you in a deal like that," and he said, "Well, can you loan me a hundred dollars? I need cash money to get up there to make this deal." And I said, "Yes, I can do that, I can do that."

And I got my billfold and I gave him a hundred dollar bill, and he went up there to Pikeville, and he walked in that room with those bankers, and he made that deal. And for the next nine years we made money dealing with that hotel.

There's a lot of stories that may be told about our association with that motel in Pikeville, Kentucky. Lloyd often repeats this story to new people comin' into the hospitality industry, where he has excelled, and he often quotes this story that sometimes a hundred dollars can save your butt.

~~~

Lloyd Abdoo, center, and I with Ken Nantz, right.

I was on a trip to New York to a big antique show that was happenin' up there in New York City, and I had a pretty big amount of money on me, and I was there to buy some antique documents and such, come back home and frame 'em up and sell 'em at auction, which is what I've been doin' for the last 30 years.

So it was on one of these trips that I stopped in to see my friend Lloyd Abdoo in Pikeville, Kentucky. We had a little deal goin', and I stopped by on my way to New York to see if it was okay, and I spent the night with him. We went out to eat, and he had this limousine and he had a driver, and we went out to this place in the mountains to eat.

And on the way out there he asked me, "Do you have a thousand dollars on you?" And I said, "Yes, I do," and he said, "Can I borrow it?" And I said, "Okay."

So I took a thousand dollars out of my billfold, you know, and I gave him ten one hundred dollar bills, and he rolled 'em up real tight, and it was pourin' down rain; it was nasty and muddy up there, and we had a couple of business people from Lexington that were in the car with us, and he rolled the window down and he tossed the thousand dollars out the window.

I was so taken aback I was speechless for a few seconds, and then I came to my senses, and I told the limousine driver, "Turn this thing around and go back!" And I told Lloyd, "If we don't find that money, this time I'm goin' to kill you. I'm prepared to spend the rest of my life in prison, but I'm goin' to kill you."

So we went back and, lo and behold, that money was lying right on the edge of a mud hole. A truck or two had run over it, but what's the chances of throwing a thousand dollars out the window on a nasty, rainy night and finding it when you went back, knowing this story would be told many times.

~~~

There was a time when Lloyd and I worked at the Holiday Inn in Corbin, Kentucky. He was the manager and I was the assistant manager, and it was an adventure. They had never had anybody working for them that could equal us.

We had things happening. We were good managers, and the people in the city liked us pretty well, and we had a pretty good stint working for Winegardner Hammonds, who owned a lot of Holiday Inns up and down 75.

It was at that Holiday Inn, though, that we excelled at innovation. We were sittin' around our office one day, and this tractor trailer pulled into the parking lot, and this guy came in and asked to speak to the owner or manager of the Holiday Inn, so they directed him to Lloyd and I.

And this guy came in and told us a very sad story. He told us he had come from North Carolina to deliver a load of recliners to an establishment in Corbin, Kentucky. This was in early December. He was supposed to get a cashier's check for the load, and when he got there the man at the store didn't have a cashier's check, and the fella this guy worked for refused to take a regular check. So he was on his way back to North Carolina with this load of furniture. He had like 125 recliners on that truck.

So he wanted a particular amount – I don't remember exactly what it was, but it was a substantial amount of money, more than Lloyd or I had ever had in our pocket for several years after that. So he asked if we wanted to buy this group of recliners – it was something like ten thousand dollars, and of course we didn't have that kind of money – so we tried to determine what to do.

I hope that the statute of limitations has run out on this particular deal. There was no money lost by Holiday Inn, but we decided to buy that load of recliners and pay for it out of the petty cash from the Holiday Inn. And that's what we did. We bought that load of furniture for ten thousand dollars, and we had 125 recliners and figured we'd sell 'em at a hundred dollars each, and we'd have twenty-five hundred dollars left over.

But they sold so well we ended up making about three thousand dollars, and we were on our way. We've been entrepreneurs ever since, and the Holiday Inn never knew the difference because within about 48 hours we'd sold enough recliners to put the ten thousand dollars back into petty cash.

I often think what could've happened if we hadn't been able to sell them; they'd probably have come and put us in jail. But it was a start for us and gave us the sense that we could do anything in sales.

So from then on we were looking for ways to make money. The last year I worked for Holiday Inn I made more money selling art than in the Holiday Inn, and I've been in the art business ever since. We got our start right there at the Holiday Inn in Corbin, Kentucky.

A postscript to this story is that the next week the same guy showed up and tried to sell us a second load of recliners, and being the wise people we were – and the frightened people we became because of this deal – we sent him on down the road. We didn't buy that second load of recliners. We figured we'd made all the money we could make on that deal, and we were probably correct. But it was certainly an adventure.

~~~

As I speak, they're closin' down one of my favorite places in the world. It is called Men of Measure. It was a place to buy clothes that weren't drab; it was a place to hang out; it was a place to become friends with Augie and Jack, and for thirty years I bought clothes from those two guys at the Men of Measure. It was a friendship that developed over the years.

Early on, I came in the store one day and with all the flamboyance I could raise I walked around and we chatted a little bit, and they were having a sale. I walked around the store several times, and I was used to making offers on clothes; I never paid what they asked. I've often wondered how many people go in a clothing store and negotiate a price.

So I walked in there, and they had these silk ties; they were thirty dollar ties and they had them on sale for fifteen dollars.

So I told Jack Phillips, I said, "Jack, I will give you three dollars apiece for every tie in the store. I don't care where they're at; you go and get every tie you got here; I'll give you three dollars apiece if you give me that fixture they're on." Jack said, "Are you kiddin'?" I said, "No, I'm not; I'll give you three dollars for every tie you got in the joint."

So he started gathering the ties he had and maybe started to count 'em, and I said, "No, you can't count 'em. It's one of those snap decisions; you either wanna do it, or you don't."

So Jack said, "I think I'll do it." So I said, "Okay. How many ties you got?" So he went through every tie in the place, the good ones and the bad ones and piled 'em all up, and there was like three hundred and forty ties, something like that. And I ended up with, uh, fifteen hundred dollars in ties, most of 'em long ties. I kept all the red ones 'cause I'm partial to 'em; I don't wear 'em a whole lot, but I've got a lot of red ties.

As it turned out, this was really cheap, cheap notoriety cuz I never set foot in the store after that that one of the guys didn't take me around to everybody in the store at the time and say, "Meet the man who bought every tie in the place at one time."

After that Jack and I became really good friends, and I'm sad to see they're closing down the store this week. You know, big guys have to wear clothes that fit 'em; you can't go around with your pants not comin' quite high enough and your shirt not goin' quite low enough, leavin' an exposed expanse of unsightly body that nobody wants to look at. And these guys kept me dressed over the years in pretty nice clothes — nice enough to convince my wife Pat that I was a person of substance.

It was the best fifteen hundred dollars I ever spent. It was always nice to be recognized for that.

~~~

For thirteen years my wife and I have been members of the Farragut Lions Club. During that time we've run into many, many wonderful personalities. Everybody in the Lions Club has a very distinctive personality, and we all blend in together to make a pretty funny group.

Now there was a man in our group who was sixty-five years old. To my knowledge, he had never been married, and he was a wonderful fella and a founding member of the Farragut Lions Club. His family was all gone, and he was kinda left alone, and he had some health issues, and one night he was driving and happened into the less desirable district of Knoxville by accident.

So he came up to a red light, and this young lady of the evening knocked on his window, and he rolled down his window, and she says, "Come with me. I will do anything you want me to do for two hundred dollars. Anything."

He looked at her and said, "Anything? You'll do anything I wanna have done for two hundred dollars?" And she said, "Yes, I will do that," and he said, "Well, jump in. We'll go paint my house."

~~~

My best friend Lloyd Abdoo had cancer, and I took time off every couple of weeks to go up and visit him. He lived in Carrollton, Kentucky, which is halfway between Cincinnati and Louisville on Interstate 71.

Just across the river from where Lloyd had three hotels and where his house was was a barge in Madison, Indiana, where there was a casino. This was a beautiful place, and they had a five-star restaurant in that casino, and Lloyd and I happened to know the fellow who owned it.

So we went across for dinner and we had perhaps the best dinner we'd ever had in our life, Pat and I decided. After the dinner, Theresa went to play some slot machines and Pat went with her, and I went with Lloyd to this room where he and I and a dealer were playing blackjack.

Well, I'm not a gambler but Lloyd plays blackjack and has won many dollars over his career playing blackjack. He took $5,000 out of his bank account, and the casino had a bank and after about three hours he'd won thirty-seven hundred dollars. So he took out five hundred dollars of that eighty-seven hundred, and he put the rest of it back in the bank.

So he took the five hundred dollars and he purchased five coins at a hundred dollars each that went into the slot machines. Then he took me into this special room with slot machines in there, and each play was a hundred dollars. So he had these five hundred dollar coins, and he gave 'em to me and he said, "Pick out a slot machine and put the coin in and pull the handle."

So I did that, and bells and whistles went off and blue lights, and everybody in the place came to see what was goin' on, and I had won fifteen hundred dollars, the first time and the only time I'd ever put money into a slot machine.

So I had five coins, and I picked out a second machine and I put a coin and pulled the handle, and nothin' happened. I was disappointed that nothin' happened, and I knew that I could get addicted to playin' these slot machines. I knew I was never gonna do this again, so I put the third coin in and pulled the handle, and I won a thousand dollars.

I thought maybe Lloyd had rigged this to surprise me but he had not. It was just the biggest surprise of my life; I'd won twice out of three times.

So I picked another machine and I put in a coin and I pulled the handle and I didn't win anything. There was a machine there that Lloyd had won a lot of money from at a previous time, so I asked where that machine was and I went over and put my last coin in that machine, and I won five hundred dollars.

So I won three out of five times. I did not want to take any of the money, but he insisted that I take half the money. So I gave Pat seven hundred fifty dollars and I kept seven hundred fifty dollars and I told her to put it in her pocketbook and we'd do something frivolous with it or something down the road. And I did the same with mine expect for a hundred dollars; I gave a hundred dollars to Philip who works for me, because Lloyd always gives him a hundred dollars when he sees him.

So anyway, we were up in Philadelphia at David Lochman's house. I'd just bought a group of first-edition King James Bible leaves from him, and I'd spent quite a bit of money with him, and he wanted me to give him a couple thousand dollars in cash. I told him I was goin' to report it, and he said, "That's OK, I'd just like to have the cash." I said, "Well, I don't have it on me, you know, I'm goin' up to New England to buy some other paper and I need to hold onto my cash, so you just hang onto what I've bought here, and when I get home I'll send you a cashier's check." He said, "No, no, no, we've done business before and I know who you are."

But then I thought of this money we had stashed. I asked Pat if she still had her seven hundred fifty dollars, and she said she did; and I knew I still had my six hundred fifty dollars, so I put a little money with it and I was able to give him the two thousand dollars cash he asked me for.

So when I got home, I told my pastor, David Garnett, this story, and I asked him, was I gonna be all right with it, and he said yep, he thought I did good with the money and it was all legitimate. That has to be some kind of a record, to win three times out of five. That can get you addicted, and I vowed that I wouldn't do that again.

Best friends for 40 years: from left, Ken Nantz, Colan Harell, Lloyd Abdoo, Zafer Roback, and me, seated.

MULE STORY NUMBER TWO

Everyone from Possum Trot had a mule story. I would be remiss if I did not have one also.

One night there was a young fellow driving up through Possum Trot. There was about six inches of snow on the ground, and he ran off the road into the ditch. And he tried to get the car out for some time, and decided he couldn't do it, so he started to look around for something or somebody to help him.

So he saw a light way out in the field, and he trotted through the snow and the ice to a farmer's house way out there, and he knocked on the door, and the ol' farmer came out, and he asked him, "Do you have a tractor, sir?" And he said, "No, I don't have a tractor. How can I help you?"

And he said, "Well, my car's run off the road down there in the ditch, and I can't get it out."

And the ol' farmer said, "Well, hold on a minute, let me get Ol' Henry and we'll see if we can get your car out of the ditch." And the fellow said, "Well, who's Ol' Henry," and he said, "Ol' Henry's my mule." "Can he pull a car out of the ditch by himself?" "Well, we'll go see."

So they harnessed up Ol' Henry and hitched him up to the car, and the farmer said, "Get up, Henry! Get up, John! Get up, Bill!" And Henry took a lunge and set that car back up on the road.

The young fellow was amazed, and he said to the farmer, "I really have to ask you, you called out two or three names. What was that about?" And the farmer said, "Well, you see, Ol' Henry's blind, but if he thinks he's part of a team, he can do anything."

APPENDICES

THINGS I'VE LEARNED ALONG THE WAY

Your home should be a haven for friends passing through.

Hate no one.

Susie said, "It is better to want what you get, than to get what you want."

A life without service to others is wasted.

Don't shoot a skunk too close to the barn.

Art soothes the soul after a hard day's work.

When a door closes, another opens.

I am proud to be a graduate of University of the Cumberlands "where all the Indians are Patriots".

Just do what you can.

If I were giving a speech on the five people who have influenced me, I would be sure those five were alive and in the audience.

Give your belongings away while you are alive and can enjoy the giving.

As I get older, having the correct change is more important than the line forming behind me while I try to locate it somewhere in my car.

Get to know your neighbors.

Know your doctors and make them your friends.

Wear ties that have red in them.

If you should be overweight, wear clothes that fit you.

Love your parents.

A good education takes a lifetime.

Choice of art defines a man.

Live your life in such a way that the church is full and running over at your funeral.

Have a lot of friends, but only a couple of best friends.

Getting old is not for wimps.

Enjoy your work.

Choose your friends carefully.

Don't question another man's prices – he has his reasons; just make an offer.

Friends from womb to tomb.

In the long run, price is not important, terms are.

Over the years, small contributions add up.

Never forget who "brung" you to the dance.

The value of art consists not in the artist but in the work of art.

Willy said, "You could use used material in building if you did it in workman order."

It has been said that Einstein's last words were "not by chance."

Always vote, because not voting may indeed be a vote.

Evil cannot overcome good.

Time heals all wounds, and time wounds all heels.

As you make your way through life, you will no doubt accumulate things that seem important to you. Do not leave those treasured items for someone else to distribute – distribute these items yourself so as to enjoy the pleasure of giving.

One of Joe's great questions was "who walked through the mud puddles on the way back from school today?" We always told him the truth. "It was those Sullivan girls."

You do not have to have water to have a yacht club.

My mother wrote this piece for the London, Ky., newspaper, and I've always found it to be inspirational.

The Free and The Brave
By Susan Lipps

I have been in love with America all my life. American history reads like a romance to me. As we study the lives of American giants, such as Franklin, Washington, Hamilton, and Jefferson, we cannot help but love and revere them. But, there were men of lesser stature who also left their mark on our history pages. Such a man was Francis Scott Key.

He came from Maryland and had a fine family background. He was of a poetic nature. Key was involved in church work all his life, and was also a lawyer.

Key was 25 years old in September, 1814, when he was sent on a mission to secure the release of an American doctor from a British ship in the Chesapeake Bay. America was at war with Great Britain again. The British Army had burned Washington and now the British Navy was in Chesapeake Bay, preparing to storm Fort McHenry and capture Baltimore.

Key secured the release of the doctor but they were both detained as the battle was about to begin. He spent a harrowing night on the ship, but his fine, sensitive mind created from the experience a poem which gives a superlative visual image and has made millions of

Americans through the years tingle with emotion. Whenever I hear "The Star-Spangled Banner," I get so many cross currents of emotion that the tears begin to well up in my eyes, and I am not ashamed of this.

Some people think it is not fashionable to be emotional about our flag. But our flag is the token of our country. If we love and revere America, we must also love and revere our flag. In the light made by the fire from the bombs, Key watched for our flag and composed the following:

Oh, say, can you see, by the dawn's early light,
What so proudly we hailed at the twilight's last gleaming?
Whose broad stripes and bright stars in the perilous fight
O'er the ramparts we watched, were so gallantly streaming.
And the rockets' red glare, the bombs bursting in air,
Gave proof through the night that our flag was still there.
Oh, say, does that star-spangled banner yet wave
O'er the land of the free and the home of the brave?

Since the beginning of our nation, we have been free and brave, each succeeding generation in its own way. Our precious flag is the symbol that gives hope to people all over the world. It represents a dream. We all know that we have flaws here and there, but our history abounds with splendid men who had great vision. They have had heart, strength and warmth.

Yes, this is the land of the free and the home of the brave. America, oh, how I love you!

THE FAMILIES OF POSSUM TROT, 1960

Bill Wilson Family

Lucy Jackson Family

Clyde Sullivan Family

Waymon Weaver Family

Oliver Smith Family

Ada Smith Family

Joe Lipps Family

Richmond Hammock Family

Willie Langdon Family

John Lipps Family

Nate Clibern Family

Clayton Williams Family

Glen Williams Family

Jerry Overbay Family

Virgil Overbay Family

Jones Family

George Bradly Family

Bill Smith Family

Early Family

Homer Day Family

Balton Rush Family

Earl Coffey Family

PEOPLE WHO HAVE INFLUENCED MY LIFE OR JUST WANTED THEIR NAME IN A BOOK

Abdoo, Frank	Brewer., Randle
Abdoo, Lloyd	Brome, Dr. John
Abdoo, Teresa	Brooks, Pam
Akers, Eddie	Burrow, Kathy
Alexander, Kurt	Burrow, Norvell
Alexander, Susan	Casey, Don
Armstrong, Connie	Casey, Lucile
Armstrong, Dr. David	Coffee, Dennis
Beck, Alicia	Colegrove, Mike
Bentley, Mr.	Crail, Mary Lou
Bergman, Dave	Crawford, Clare
Bland, John	Crawford, Dave
Boswell, Dr. J. M.	Crutchfield, Gerri
Bradley, George	Duke, Dr. John
Brady, Earl	Duncan, Mike
Brewer, Dr. Michelle	Dunn, Larry

Dunn, Maureen

Evans, Mrs.

Fisher, Marcia

Fisher, Paul

Fleenor, Rick

Freeman, Bill

Fugate, Bob

Garnett, Molly

Garnett, Rev. David

Gilliam, Carolyn

Glass, Ron

Gregory, Coach Joe Tom

Greiwe, Nick

Hammock, Orville

Hammock, Richmond

Harrell, Colan

Hart, Jim

Hart, Julia

Hatton, Mr.

Hendrix, Dr. Craig

Hennie, Dr. Craig

Henson, Ruby

Hollingsworth, Vicki Skeen

Hubbard, Harold

Ison, Dr. David

Jackson, Willis

Jarvis, Dan

Jarvis, Jody

Kendrick, Jo

Killion, Gene

Koeniger, Dick

Langdon, Willie

Leonard, Carl

Lipps, Abner

Lipps, Connie Leggett

Lipps, Elaine Perkins

Lipps, Joe

Lipps, Patricia Skeen Artman

Lipps, Ralph

Lipps, Susie

Lowe, Philip

Lynch, Ralph

Mahler, Marty

Mee, Ed

Mee, Sandy

Miller, Bobbie

Miller, Jack

Minton, Dennis

Minton, Sue

Miracle Telvis

Mullins, Ronald

Myers, Helen

Nantz, Ken

Napier, Ronald

Nunn, Gov. Louie

Peters, Mr. Arthur

Petrey, Dr. Carolyn

Petrey, Dr. Dallas

Phillips, Jack

Prater, Ken

Raaf, Adolph

Raaf, Sue

Raby, Ann

Renfro, Jim

Rice, Dr. Allen

Roback, Zafer

Roberts, Bruce

Roberts, Mary

Sain, Riley

Sain, Sue

Sasser, Mr.

Scott, Jackie

Sesler, Mart

Sherman, Dr. Phil

Sherman, Sandy

Shireman, Jonathan

Shireman, Pat

Shoudy, Howard

Shoudy, Joyce

Siler, Judge Gene

Skeen, Jack

Skeen, Jack (Chip)

Slyman, Jim

Steely, Paul

Stephens, Fletcher

Stephens, Joe

Stephens, Katherine

Sterling, Kimball

Stormer, Marty

Stormer, Wayne

Sullivan, Clyde

Tackett, John

Taylor, Dinah

Taylor, Dr. Jim

Thomas, Pat

Thomas, Rev. Eugene

Thompson, Dr. Don

Thompson, Janet

Thompson, Kay

Trout, Dr. Monroe

Trout, Sandra

Truman, Dan

Truman, Donnie

Vernon, Randy

Wake, Dr. Eric

Wake, Sue

Warren, Rev. Jonathan

Warren, Siobhan

Weaver, Mrs.

White, Bob

White, Dan

White, Donna

White, Margaret

White, Russ

* If your name does not appear above, let me know and I'll put you in my next book.

Vote for

Abner Lipps - President
Ray Lipps - Vice-President
of the
Men's Council

Election will be from
1:00 until 6:00 P.M. Wednesday
on the
Gangway at the Entrance
to North Hall

My first venture into politics, at Cumberland College

The Honorable Order of
Kentucky Colonels
INCORPORATED
A Non-Profit Charitable Organization

NATIONAL HEADQUARTERS • THE FOREST • ANCHORAGE, KENTUCKY

Colonel Roy Lips   July 7, 1969
Route 4
London, Kentucky

Dear Colonel Lips:

    We have recently been informed by our Commander-in-Chief, Governor Louie B. Nunn, that you have been appointed as Aide-de-Camp on his Staff with the rank of Colonel.

    This appointment has automatically made you a member of the Honorable Order of Kentucky Colonels binding together all Kentucky Colonels of the past and present into an organization that expresses the pride they feel in their Commission and association with others similarly honored. The first appointment of a Colonel by a Governor of Kentucky was made by Governor Isaac Shelby and dates back to the year 1812.

    It is our pleasure to enclose your 1969 membership card.

    Upon request, I will be glad to send additional information in order to bring you up to date on your organization matters.

    We are enclosing a card which we would appreciate your sending back to us giving us the address where you would like to receive your future membership cards and other communications.

        Sincerely,

        Colonel Anna Friedman Goldman
        Colonel Anna Friedman Goldman
        Secretary and Keeper of the Great Seal
        The Honorable Order of Kentucky Colonels

AFG/mm

College
Republican
National
Committee.

August 25, 1970

Chairman
Robert Polack

Co-Chairman
Helen Krvavica

Vice Chairman
Joseph Abate

Vice Chairman
Michael Organ

Secretary
Lynn Erickson

Treasurer
Steve Dreisier

Executive Director
Morton Blackwell

Ray Lipps
c/o Office of the Dean of Admissions
Cumberland College
Willaimsburg, Kentucky

Dear Ray:

It is my pleasure to appoint you Chairman of the Club Intra-
Communications and Publicity Committee of the College Republican
National Committee.

With the ever increasing growth in membership at the local College
Republican club level, the rapid development of CR organizational
and programming ideas and technique and of student campaigning
technique and the need for a moderate voice on the nation's campuses,
the need and opportunity for good communication among College
Republican club members and between the campus College Republican
club and the academic community has never been greater. Yours is
a big responsibility, a job that needs to be done. I am very much
looking forward to working with you.

Please send me a job description of the activities and programs
you intend the Club Intra-Communications and Publicity Committee
to initiate and accomplish.

Welcome to the CRNC.

Warm personal regards,

Robert Polack,
Chairman

RP/skj

National Headquarters: 1625 Eye Street NW Washington DC 20006 (202) NA 8-6800.

CUMBERLAND COLLEGE

J.M. Boswell
President Emeritus

July 2, 1985

Mr. Ray Lipps
Tattersall Trails, End Drive
Corbin, Kentucky 40701

Dear Ray,

I deeply appreciate your coming by my office. I have written a
letter to Denise. She is a young person with a great future. She has
evidently learned how to apply herself to her studies. Moreover, she
has a very strong academic background. I think there is no question
but that she will do well as a college student.

One of the greatest services an alumnus can render for Cumberland
College is to recommend students. You are doing your part in this
respect, in addition, you are contributing financially, and, also, you
are talking to others about Cumberland College. This is great.

I am dictating this letter before I talk with Ralph. If he does
not call me today, I will telephone him.

I thank you again for your continuing loyalty to and support of
Cumberland College. I deeply appreciate your friendship and your personal
loyalty to me.

Sincerely,

J. M. Boswell

J. M. Boswell
President Emeritus

JMB/dlp

145

Draughons Junior College

Dewitt Shelton
President

315 Erin Drive
Knoxville, Tennessee 37919
Phone 615/584-8621

October 19, 1987

Mr. Ray Lipps
Esquire Trading Company
304 Northshore Drive
Knoxville, TN 37919

Dear Mr. Lipps:

On behalf of Draughons Junior College, I would like to express our appreciation for your delivery of the commencement address last Thursday evening. Our faculty, administration, and graduates have commented that this was "the best speaker ever". Your thoughts were well received as I was confident they would be.

Ray, I would like to say a personal thank you for taking time out, and cutting your well-deserved vacation short to come and motivate our graduates.

Sincerely,

DRAUGHONS JUNIOR COLLEGE

Donna J. Brady

Donna J. Brady
Employment Director

DJB/tg

Accredited by –
THE ASSOCIATION OF INDEPENDENT COLLEGES AND SCHOOLS
Washington, D.C.

146

CUMBERLAND COLLEGE

WILLIAMSBURG, KENTUCKY 40769-1372
PHONE (606) 549-2200
OFFICE OF THE PRESIDENT

October 19, 1992

Mr. Ray Lipps
7632 Clinton Highway
Powell, Tennessee 37849

Dear Ray,

I'm writing this letter to thank you for every kindness you have extended and continue to extend to Cumberland College.

You've served us well as President of our Alumni Association, and I think the standing ovation given to you was a small indication of the esteem with which you are held.

Secondly I want to thank Bella, too, for the clear love she demonstrates for the college. The prints you framed are simply beautiful, and I want you both to see them and soon.

By-the-way, you were more than gracious to fly to Detroit to appraise Blair's Christmas Land Collection which is now domiciled safely in the Cumberland Museum. You made it possible! Incidentally your speech was not only tremendous but also accurate in detail. I thought I should stand and politely deny that I was a "hustler" because I was working with a lady on a gift who was in the audience and I didn't want her to think I was doing what I was doing, and I knew you could well understand.

Nevertheless, Ray, we are proud of you, proud of your entire family, and we feel you reflect immense credit on Cumberland College.

With warmest regards, I am

Cordially,

Jim Taylor
President

JT/seg

147

June 17, 2005

RAY LIPPS
POWELL, TN

Dear Melvin Jones Fellow:

On behalf of Lions Clubs International Foundation, we congratulate you on being named a Melvin Jones Fellow.

The Melvin Jones Fellowship honors Melvin Jones, the founder of Lions Clubs International. It is the highest form of recognition conferred by the foundation. It is largely due to the growth of the fellowship program that LCIF has been able to meet humanitarian needs in communities worldwide. In many cases these needs are reflected in the eyes of disadvantaged children. Or perhaps made apparent by a common sense of hopelessness shared by the elderly whose community has been unable to care for them. LCIF continually meets needs such as these through the generosity of Lions, and others, who have contributed to the Melvin Jones Fellowship Program.

As a Melvin Jones Fellow, your name has been added to our listing of all individuals in the program. These names are electronically shown in continuous rotation in the LCIF Recognition Room at International Headquarters. This exhibit stands as a tribute to a growing network of individuals who are committed to the humanitarian objectives of LCIF.

I urge you to wear your Melvin Jones Fellow lapel pin with pride. It represents your dedication to making the world a better place through humanitarian service.

Yours truly,

Dr. Tae-Sup Lee
Chairperson, Board of Trustees

LCIF-3 English 1/2007GB

SIGHTFIRST

300 West 22nd Street, Oak Brook, Illinois 60523-8842, USA   Phone 630-571-5466   Fax 630-571-5735

148

"Producing Tomorrow's Servant Leaders of Character Today with Warm Hearts, Keen Minds, Helping Hands"

January 19, 2011

Dr. Ray Lipps
4419 Cornview Lane
Knoxville, Tennessee 37938

Dear Dr. Ray,

Here is a picture of the Lincoln print about which we chatted briefly. The fellow is asking outrageous amounts to get a copy of the print. My purpose is inquiring about getting it or something similar to it is to use it next February (2012) as a premium in a mailout (we will need around 5,000). As time permits you may have some ideas of what could be done to get something similar at substantially less cost per print.

Needless to say, I've heard nothing but glowing and stellar remarks about the honorary degree ceremony. Everyone was so pleased. Thanks, too, for the spectacular art work, the $950.19 in coins, the matching fund from Lloyd Abdoo and for every other act of kindness. By-the-way, your brother and my new brother-in-law said he would also match the amount each year.

Dr. Ray, you are number one in our estimation and this is verified by the exceedingly and unusually large number of family and friends who attended the ceremony.

By the way, Paris Hopkins and his wife wanted to attend and sent word but were inadvertently absent.

Office of the President, 6191 College Station Drive, Williamsburg, KY 40769
Phone: 606-539-4201 • Fax: 606-549-2820 • Email: presoff@ucumberlands.edu • www.ucumberlands.edu

UNIVERSITY of the CUMBERLANDS
Cumberland College
Since 1888

*"Producing Tomorrow's Servant Leaders of Character Today
with Warm Hearts, Keen Minds, Helping Hands"*

October 7, 2013

Dr. and Mrs. Ray Lipps
4419 Cornview Lane
Knoxville, Tennessee 37938

Dear Ray and Pat,

I'm so pleased we had the opportunity to honor both of you – an honor all too long in coming!

The number of friends who gathered to celebrate with you is no small indication of the wealth you have in family and friends.

Indeed, the Trouts came to honor you – quite a testimony!

Thanks, too for the nice things you said about Dinah and me.

You are always so thoughtful, and we are thankful.

Sincerely,

Jim Taylor
President

JT/sr

Office of the President, 6191 College Station Drive, Williamsburg, KY 40769
Phone: 606-539-4201 • Fax: 606-539-4260 • Email: presoff@ucumberlands.edu • www.ucumberlands.edu

150

Made in the USA
Middletown, DE
08 August 2016